Contents

ABOVE: They can't believe what they are seeing – like many, many more Londoners who were shocked, surprised and delighted to see a steam train running alongside their standard tube service, and hurriedly scrambled for cameras to record the moment. Metropolitan Railway E class 0-4-4-T is seen on arrival at Farringdon with one of the Met 150 specials on January 13, 2013. ANDY BARR

FRONT COVER MAIN PICTURE: Metropolitan Railway E class 0-4-4T No. 1 makes a spirited departure from Earls Court on August 2, 2014, during the Hammersmith & City 150 celebrations. JOHN TITLOW

FRONT COVER RIGHT: Ancient and modern side by side at Euston Square. JOHN TITLOW

FRONT COVER MIDDLE: The Metropolitan Railway's coat of arms. ANDY BARR

FRONT COVER LEFT: No.1 storms through Paddington Underground station on January 13, 2013, with a Metropolitan Railway 150th anniversary special. JOHN TITLOW

STEAM ON THE **UNDERGROUND**

AUTHOR: Robin Jones

DESIGN: atg-media.com

PRODUCTION EDITOR: Sarah Palmer

COVER DESIGN: Michael Baumber

REPROGRAPHICS: Jonathan Schofield

MARKETING MANAGER: Charlotte Park

PUBLISHER: Tim Hartley

COMMERCIAL DIRECTOR: Nigel Hole

PUBLISHING DIRECTOR: Dan Savage

PUBLISHED BY: Mortons Media Group Ltd, Media Centre, Morton Way, Horncastle, Lincolnshire, LN9 6JR
Tel: 01507 529529

PRINTED BY: William Gibbons And Sons, Wolverhampton

CREDITS: All pictures marked * are published under a Creative Commons licence. Full details may be obtained at http://creativecommons.org/licences

ISBN: 978-1-909128-68-2

MORTONS MEDIA GROUP LTD

Introduction

This special publication offers not one, but three, major stories about London and indeed Britain's ground-breaking railway history and heritage.

Firstly, when Britain launched the world's first underground city line, in the form of the Metropolitan Railway in 1863, it set a standard for others to follow. And for the first few decades of its operation, steam, not electric, traction hauled trains of both passengers and freight through the tunnels.

Secondly, the history of steam traction on the Underground is told in full, from those earliest times to 1971. That was when, three years after steam haulage ended on the British Rail network, London Underground dispensed with the services of its last steam locomotives.

Thirdly, and most poignantly, it tells the story of how steam returned to the London Underground lines, both above and below the surface.

It began with the original Steam on the Met series, which ran from 1989-2000, and came back with a vengeance in 2013 with a national award-winning series of steam specials to mark the 150th anniversary of the first underground trains.

The ability to run a complete Victorian wooden-bodied steam train in-between regular modern electric tube services shows that London's subway system is still well ahead of the pack.

However, while the steam specials have been a true capital success, it has taken a real nationwide effort to make them happen.

Backing London Transport Museum's plans to celebrate 150 years of the Metropolitan Railway was, in the first instance, the Buckinghamshire Railway Centre at Quainton Road. Its 10-year loan agreement of Metropolitan Railway flagship E class 0-4-4T No. 1 was pivotal to the scheme.

Then came Bill Parker's Flour Mill workshop at Bream in the Forest of Dean in deepest Gloucestershire; a market leader in the overhaul and maintenance of 19th-century locomotives.

It borrowed the National Railway Museum's London & South Western Railway Beattie well tank No. 30587 from the Bodmin & Wenford Railway, and ran night-time test runs through the tunnels beneath central London to see if the project was possible. It was – and then the Flour Mill not only overhauled Met No. 1, but provided the expert crews to drive it over the Underground. Later on, the Flour Mill would create a new sub class of steam locomotive, by lowering the cab roof of its much-travelled GWR prairie tank so it could fit inside the tunnels.

The Avon Valley Railway at Bristol hosted Met No. 1 as it was being run in, and then special dispensation was granted for it to be

ABOVE: Flour Mill driver, Geoff Phelps, on the footplate of Met No. 1. The Flour Mill locomotive crews have been praised for their professionalism throughout the steam specials on the Underground. ROBIN JONES
RIGHT: Metropolitan Railway E class 0-4-4T No. 1 and GWR prairie No. 5521, now painted in maroon London Underground livery as L150, top and tail one of the Watford 90 specials to Chesham. ROBIN JONES

LEFT: Capital transport of yesteryear: Metropolitan Railway E class 0-4-4T No.1. backed by vintage electric locomotive No. 12 *Sarah Siddons*, crosses the Grand Union Canal with the 3.10pm special from Watford's Underground station to Chesham on September 12, 2015, during the Watford 90 celebrations. ROBIN JONES

ABOVE: As part of the meticulous planning for the Metropolitan Railway 150 celebrations, on February 26, 2012, Beattie well tank No. 30587 ran a test train through the tunnels to see if steam operation was possible. It is pictured at Baker Street station. ROBIN JONES
BELOW: LONDON TRANSPORT MUSEUM

tested at 50mph on the Severn Valley Railway, so it could prove that it could keep pace with the rigorous tube timetable.

Meanwhile, in the heart of Snowdonia, the Ffestiniog Railway's Boston Lodge workshops tackled their first-ever standard gauge coach restoration project on behalf of its Covent Garden museum owners. Metropolitan Railway Jubilee coach No. 353 was meticulously restored to its as-new condition to take part in the special train consist – for which the Bluebell Railway agreed to allow its four-coach Chesham set to return to the Underground.

The Epping Ongar Railway, a unique example of part of the Underground system now in private ownership and run as a heritage line, which has also scooped national honours, also played its part in the preparations, as did the Great Central Railway, which facilitated testing of the Jubilee coach at speed to see if it, too, could be run at 50mph.

Getting to know the Underground staff involved in the build-up to the 2013 big event under the leadership of mastermind Andy Barr, heritage operations manager on the tube and now at the London Transport Museum, it was obvious that they did not view their job as a nine-to-five affair, but were enthusiasts in their own right. Their dedication was mirrored by that of the splendid staff at the museum, from the superb marketing executives and administrative staff to director Sam Mullins, who all left no stone unturned to make what seemed a mission impossible, possible.

Met 150 grabbed world headlines, deservedly so, and established a template by which steam can now regularly return to the Underground, the last special event at the time of writing being the Watford 90 celebrations in September 2015.

The events have brought infinite pleasure to London residents and visitors alike, and worldwide acclaim for the railway, which has for a century and a half serviced the beating heart of the capital. London's underground was the first – and in going back to its roots in the 21st century, has again shown why it is still the best.

Robin Jones

Chapter 1

The world's first underground railway

Global history was made in 1863, when Britain led the world in unveiling the first underground railway, made possible by steam traction.

When the major railway companies planned their great London termini, they were barred from building them within the city limits.

So, in the 1850s, if you wanted to travel into the city from King's Cross, Euston, Paddington, Waterloo, Fenchurch Street, or London Bridge, or access one from the other, you either had to walk or take a horse bus, a form of road transport that was already causing congestion.

The solution was to build the world's first underground railway. Just as is the case today, it was cheaper to tunnel below ground than to

pay premium prices for city properties just to knock them down.

However, anyone who tunnelled under buildings had a legal obligation to buy them, so the only cost-effective way of building an underground railway would be to lay them in tunnels beneath roads, which would be restored for highway use on a cut-and-cover principle.

In 1851, a London City solicitor, Charles Pearson, called for cheap rail travel so that the poor could move out of the slum areas, and John Hargrave Stevens, an architect and civil engineer, produced plans for a railway in the valley of the River Fleet, then an open sewer, running beneath a new road to be built north from Farringdon Street.

Their scheme as unveiled featured a tunnel capable of accommodating eight tracks linking the Great Northern Railway north of King's Cross to stations in Farringdon Street, with a later extension to Paddington to meet the Great Western Railway.

However, neither the main line railway companies nor London City Corporation were prepared to bear the financial risks of the project, so it failed to take off.

It was followed by the Bayswater, Paddington & Holborn Bridge Railway, a planned underground line from Paddington to King's Cross joining the proposed City Terminus Company line. Unlike the Pearson-Stevens' plans, no houses would have to be knocked down. This scheme marked the beginnings of the Metropolitan Railway.

Stevens was appointed as surveyor of the line, but the company's first chairman was William Malins, who claimed credit for the idea. He saw it as the start of a city-wide underground rail system, which would solve traffic congestion once and for all.

A Parliamentary Bill for what became the North Metropolitan Railway, with a large terminus in the City itself, passed its committee stage, but lack of financial support meant it did not get a second reading. However, in 1854, a subsequent Act of Parliament allowed the building of the Metropolitan Railway.

It took six years for the money to be raised, and Pearson persuaded the City Corporation to fund it.

Railway engineer John Fowler, who went on to build the Forth Bridge, was placed in charge. The final route chosen was from Paddington to Farringdon Street via King's Cross, with the line running mainly beneath

ABOVE: Metropolitan Railway A class 4-4-0T No. 23 was built by Beyer Peacock and used on the Inner Circle services until electrification in 1905. Afterwards, it hauled suburban trains and was eventually relegated to the very rural outpost of the Brill branch, which closed in 1935, as explained in Chapter 4. Renumbered L45, it was used on engineers' trains until 1948, when it had the distinction of being the oldest working locomotive in Britain. Restored to as-built condition for the Underground centenary celebrations in 1963, it is now displayed in London Transport Museum at Covent Garden.
ROBIN JONES

Marylebone and Euston roads. Ventilation shafts were provided along the route to allow the steam from the locomotives to escape from the tunnels.

Work began in February 1860 and the railway was completed in just less than three years. Sadly, Pearson never lived to see the fruits of his labours, dying in September 1862. ▶

ABOVE: A broad gauge train conveying Metropolitan Railway shareholders on an inspection of the line on January 10, 1863, before its official opening.
LONDON TRANSPORT MUSEUM

ABOVE: The building of the Metropolitan Railway in 1861 using the cut-and-cover method. LONDON TRANSPORT MUSEUM

ABOVE: London's first-ever underground train journey sets off from Edgware Road on May 24, 1862. William Gladstone, then Chancellor of the Exchequer, and his wife, as well as Metropolitan Railway engineer (John Fowler) are among the invited party aboard contractor Smith & Knight's open wagons. This was a special private trial trip in a contractor's train on the first section of the Metropolitan Railway to be completed. LONDON TRANSPORT MUSEUM

FIRST STEAM BELOW THE STREETS

The first locomotive to run on the Metropolitan Railway – but never hauled passenger trains – was a 2-4-0 tender locomotive designed by Fowler and built by Robert Stephenson & Co in 1861 in Newcastle-upon-Tyne.

He tried to tackle the issue of fumes and smoke in the tunnels by using steam generated in the boiler by firebricks previously brought to white heat.

Nicknamed 'Fowler's Ghost', it was not deemed successful and in 1865 was sold to Isaac Watt Boulton and then to Beyer Peacock of Manchester, which scrapped it.

To accommodate both the standard gauge trains of the Great Northern Railway at King's Cross, and Isambard Kingdom Brunel's 7ft ¼in broad gauge GWR trains at Paddington, the track was three-rail mixed gauge the rail nearest the platforms being shared by both gauges.

GWR locomotive engineer, Daniel Gooch, came up with a broad gauge design of 2-4-0T locomotives to work over the line, each of them fitted with condensing apparatus to recycle the smoke and vapour that would otherwise quickly fill the tunnels.

The first six, *Bee, Mosquito, Gnat, Hornet, Locust* and *Wasp* were built by Vulcan Foundry, and the second batch – *Bey Czar, Kaiser, Khan, Mogul* and *Shah* – by Kitson & co.

ABOVE: First steam on the Met: the line's engineer John Fowler designed this broad gauge 2-4-0 tender locomotive, known as the Ghost. Built in 1861 by Robert Stephenson & Co, it never hauled passenger trains and was sold two years after the line opened. LONDON TRANSPORT MUSEUM

Using gas-lit wooden-bodied carriages, the railway opened to the public on January 10, 1863, and it was an instant hit. Around 26,500 passengers used the line every day in its first few months.

The partnership between the GWR and the Met, as the first underground line came to be popularly known, ended after a series of quarrels, and the latter began running its own trains from August 11, 1863.

The Met then turned to help from the GNR, which replaced the broad gauge trains with standard gauge rolling stock. The broad gauge was removed in 1869.

Fowler needed to replace the GWR locomotives, and ordered 18 4-4-0s from Beyer Peacock. Known as the A class, the design was adapted from that of engines supplied by the firm to the Tudela & Bilbao Railway in Spain, and were among the first locomotives to be equipped with bogies.

The exhaust from the cylinders was conveyed in large pipes to the top of the side tanks where it was condensed. However, the water in the tanks became too hot to condense the steam after around an hour, and therefore needed to be replaced with cold water.

A total of 44 of the A class was eventually bought by the Met, plus 22 examples of an improved type, the B class.

These engines were painted bright green, but after JJ Hanbury became the Met's locomotive superintendent in 1885, the livery was changed to maroon. The Metropolitan District bought 54 similar Beyer Peacock tank engines, making a total of 120 on the Underground.

The line was soon extended from both ends, and northwards via a branch from Baker Street. It reached Hammersmith in 1864, via the Hammersmith & City Railway, built with Great Western co-operation. The section between Westbourne Park and Edgware Road was owned by the GWR.

Meanwhile, also in 1864, the building of the separate and very competitive Metropolitan District Railway had been officially sanctioned, with the aim of completing an 'inner circle' within London.

Conceived by John Fowler, and with several Metropolitan Railway directors on its board, it was to run via the Thames Embankment from South Kensington to Tower Hill, and connect at both ends with extensions of the Met.

The first stretch, between South Kensington and Westminster Bridge, opened on December 24, 1868, and the District line reached Blackfriars in 1870 and Mansion House in 1871.

The Met extended in stages to link up with it, reaching Moorgate Street on December 23, 1865, Bishopsgate (now Liverpool Street) on July 12, 1875 and Aldgate on November 18, 1875.

ABOVE: A recreation in London Transport Museum of the construction of the early tube tunnels. ROBIN JONES

LEFT: A 7mm scale model of the Metropolitan Railway's Edgware Road station just before opening in 1963. In the foreground is broad gauge 2-4-0T Locus while to the left is a standard gauge Hercules 4-4-0T No. 18, which has condensing apparatus for use in the tunnels. BROAD GAUGE SOCIETY

ABOVE: Metropolitan Railway A class Beyer Peacock 4-4-0T No. 2 of 1862. It is fitted with Smith's simple vacuum brake; the photograph was taken no later than 1893 when an automatic vacuum brake was introduced. The driver and fireman pose on the locomotive. LONDON TRANSPORT MUSEUM

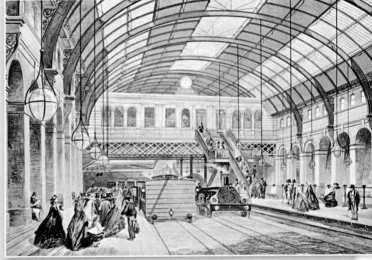

ABOVE: King's Cross Underground station around 1863. The print shows a Great Western Railway broad gauge condensing 2-4-0T and carriages on the mixed gauge track. LONDON TRANSPORT MUSEUM

ABOVE: Metropolitan Railway C class 0-4-4T No. 69 at Baker Street station around 1900. LONDON TRANSPORT MUSEUM

An extension to Richmond was opened on October 1, 1877, using the tracks of the London & South Western Railway via Hammersmith (Grove Road) to Ravenscourt Park, four months after the Metropolitan District had opened its own service to Richmond using a connection over the LSWR tracks from its Hammersmith station, which had opened three years earlier. The Met ran its Richmond service until December 31, 1906.

ABOVE: Beyer Peacock A class 4-4-0T No. 23 of 1866. LONDON TRANSPORT MUSEUM

It was not until October 6, 1884 that the Inner Circle was finally opened throughout to traffic after it was completed by the Met and the Metropolitan District.

ABOVE: Metropolitan District Railway 4-4-0T No. 38, built in 1883. LONDON TRANSPORT MUSEUM

ABOVE: A single-carriage train hauled by Metropolitan District 4-4-0T No. 41, at Wood Siding on the Brill branch in 1935. LONDON TRANSPORT MUSEUM

ABOVE: A contemporary diagram of the Metropolitan Railway at the junction of Tottenham Court Road and Hampstead Road. ILLUSTRATED LONDON NEWS

LONGER LINE, BIGGER ENGINES

After railway magnate Sir Edward Watkin became the chairman of the Met, it was transformed from being a subterranean city people carrier into a railway that would penetrate deep into the rural shires west of London.

The short Metropolitan & St John's that Railway and a branch of the Met which ran from Baker Street to Swiss Cottage, and opened in 1868, running north from Baker Street, extended in stages out into the Middlesex countryside towards the Chilterns to become the Metropolitan's main line, stimulating the development of new suburbs. Harrow-on-the-Hill was reached in 1880, and the line was extended in 1894 to Verney Junction in Buckinghamshire, more than 50 miles from Baker Street and the heart of London.

By then, the Met not only offered underground commuter services, but express passenger trains, a sizeable freight and parcels traffic, and even Pullman cars. It was more like a main line railway than an urban rapid-transit route.

An expanded empire called for more powerful engines, but the only departure from the 4-4-0T design came with five 0-6-0Ts built by the Worcester Engine Company for the 2¾-mile Metropolitan & St John's Wood Railway. Designed by Met engineer RH Burnett for the steeply graded line, his successor, J Tomlinson, took the view that the 4-4-0s could do the job just as well, and so the five were sold, four to the Taff Vale Railway and one to the Sirhowy Railway.

Watkin was also chairman of the South Eastern Railway, and in 1891 introduced four C class inside-cylindered 0-4-4Ts of a type designed by James Stirling for that railway and built by Neilson & Co of Glasgow. They were all rebuilt with new boilers between 1901-03.

Six members of a D class appeared on the Met in 1895. These Sharp Stewart 2-4-0s were of a type supplied to the Barry Railway. Two were used on the Aylesbury to Verney Junction section and four were fitted with condensing gear for use between Baker Street and Aylesbury. However, it was found that they were not powerful enough for passenger services and were used mainly on freight workings.

In 1896, locomotive superintendent TS Raney retired and was succeeded by TF Clark, who had been foreman of the locomotive shops since 1893.

He designed the E class 0-4-4Ts, of which more can be read in Chapter 7.

They were followed in 1901 by the F class 0-6-2T which, wheel arrangement apart, were similar to the E class. However, the Fs did not have steam heating equipment and were used for freight.

METROPOLITAN RAILWAY AND CONNECTIONS

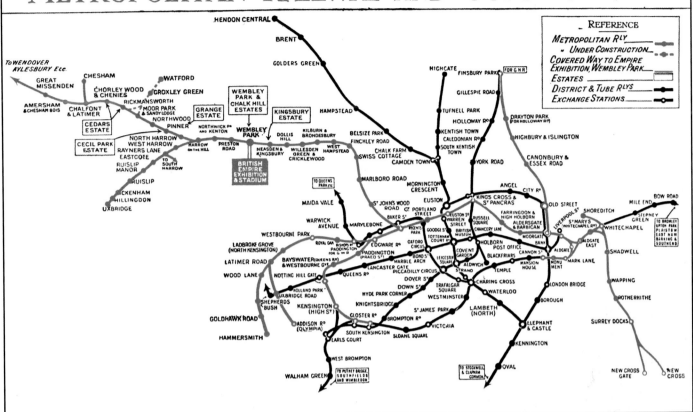

Clark's successor, Charles Jones, designed an 0-6-4T type that was bigger than anything that had worked on the Met before. The four members of the G class, like the Fs also built by the Yorkshire Engine Company, were named *Robert H. Selbie* after the railway's general manager, *Lord Aberconway* after the line's chairman, *Charles Jones* and *Brill*, reflecting, as we will see in Chapter 4, the furthest outpost of the Met.

Jones then came up with the eight members of the H class, 4-4-4T fast passenger locomotives, built by Kerr Stuart which debuted between 1920-21.

The last class was the 2-6-4T Ks. These were built from unused parts of a batch of South Eastern & Chatham Railway-designed 2-6-0 tender locomotives that the government had ordered to keep staff at Woolwich Arsenal employed after the First World War.

These were powerful freight locomotives, but had the advantage over the G class of a shorter wheelbase and so could therefore enter all of the Met's sidings.

After George Hally became the Met's Chief Mechanical Engineer in 1923, he found that by adding new side tanks, bunkers, cabs and rear bogies, he could use the parts from the unbuilt 2-6-0s to create new locomotives at half the cost of having them supplied by a manufacturer. Armstrong Whitworth supplied the extra necessary parts.

In 1933, the London Transport Passenger Board 'nationalised' the Met as a new umbrella body for the capital's by-then expansive network of tube lines, tram routes and buses.

The Metropolitan Line was the odd man out of the tube system for only nine of its 34 stations are underground, and so more than half of its routes lay in country areas outside the direct jurisdiction of the new body.

In 1937, responsibility for steam working was transferred to the London & North ▶

ABOVE: Metropolitan Railway D class Sharp Stewart 2-4-0T No. 75. LONDON TRANSPORT MUSEUM

ABOVE: In its later identity as London Transport L50, Metropolitan Railway F class 0-6-2T, built by the Yorkshire Engine Company in 1901, stands at Neasden depot. The last survivor of this class, L52, was withdrawn in 1962. LONDON TRANSPORT MUSEUM

Eastern Railway. Four G class engines, eight
Hs and six Ks went to the LNER, which took
over responsibility for passenger services
north of Rickmansworth.

The remaining steam locomotives in
London Transport ownership were given
new numbers with an L prefix, after a pair
of Hunslet 0-6-0Ts used for shunting and
engineers' trains, L30 and L31, arrived on the
District Line in 1931. ●

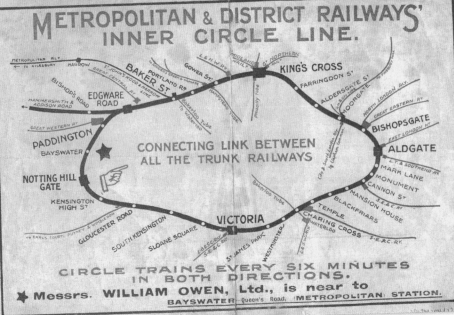

ABOVE: The Metropolitan Railway bought Peckett 0-6-0ST No. 101 in 1897 for freight transfer work, and a second, No. 102, two years later. They saw service at Finchley and Harrow-on-the-Hill. Under London Transport, they became L53 and L54, and were withdrawn in 1961 and 1962 respectively. L53 is pictured shunting at Neasden in 1957. LONDON TRANSPORT MUSEUM

BELOW AND RIGHT: One of a pair of two Hunslet 0-6-0Ts built for the Central London Railway in 1899, to a cut-down loading gauge so that they could fit inside the tube's tunnels. They were fitted with condensing gear apparatus. LONDON TRANSPORT MUSEUM

ABOVE: Metropolitan Railway A class 4-4-0T at Aldgate in 1902. LONDON TRANSPORT MUSEUM

Chapter 2

The conquest of
Metro-land

The Metropolitan Railway opened up the surrounding rural shires for commuters who wanted to make money from the City, but not to live in it.

ABOVE: Metropolitan Railway H class outside-cylindered 4-4-4T ascends Chorleywood bank in Hertfordshire with a six-coach train. LONDON TRANSPORT MUSEUM

The enterprising Metropolitan Railway quickly saw the potential for far bigger profits way beyond London's tube tunnels.

However, unlike the North London Railway, which turned the countryside to the east of London into docklands and areas of heavy industry, the Met tapped into the market of well-to-do commuters who wanted to make their money out of the city, but not live in it, and were prepared to commute from further away if fast trains were available.

Thy Met's publicity department come up with a series of stunning posters, now considered works of art, extolling the virtues of the rural paradises that the company's trains

served, far from the madding crowds of the likes of Baker Street and Paddington.

In turn, housebuilders watched with glee as the Met spread out into north-west London, Middlesex, Hertfordshire and Buckinghamshire, and were only to pleased to concrete over the golden pastures for rich dividends.

James Garland, who worked in the publicity department, dreamed up the brand name Metro-land to describe the extension of the world's first underground railway into unashamedly overground territory.

Accordingly, Metro-land, which conveyed images of a rustic Garden of Eden, with fields of grazing cows, half-timbered buildings and

olde-worlde country inns, was widely used in advertisements and promotional material from 1915 to 1934.

An annual guide called Metro-Land was published by the railway from 1915 to 1932 with the aim of promoting not only leisure and commuter travel but residency in the green shires it served. The words 'Live in Metro-land' were even etched on the door handles of the company's carriages.

A special edition of the guide was brought out in 1924 for the British Empire exhibition at the new Wembley stadium – a year after it had been used for the FA Cup final for the first time.

Harrow-on-the-Hill – considered to be the 'capital' of Metro-land, was reached in 1880.

METRO-LAND

PRICE ONE PENNY

A GOOD MOVE

— TO HARROW GARDEN VILLAGE

21 MINUTES FROM BAKER STREET. HOUSES OF VARYING TYPE BUILT BY WELL-KNOWN BUILDERS AVAILABLE AT POPULAR PRICES. LIBERAL OPEN SPACES, TENNIS COURTS, ETC. EXCELLENT SITES FOR HOUSES AND SHOP PLOTS IN COMMANDING POSITIONS. FULL PARTICULARS FROM H. GIBSON, GENERAL OFFICES, BAKER ST. STATION. CHEAP TICKETS FROM ALL METRO. STATIONS ON THURSDAYS, SATURDAYS AND SUNDAYS TO RAYNERS LANE (FOR HARROW) ADJOINING ESTATE

'FISHING' IN METRO-LAND

FULL PARTICULARS CAN BE OBTAINED FROM COMMERCIAL MANAGER, BAKER ST. STATION. N.W.1.

ABOVE AND BELOW: LONDON TRANSPORT MUSEUM COLLECTION

METROPOLITAN RAILWAY.

Visit the Glorious Countryside Served by the "Metro"

DAY and HALF DAY EXCURSIONS

SEE HANDBILLS FOR FULL PARTICULARS OR OBTAIN INFORMATION DIRECT FROM COMMERCIAL MANAGER, BAKER ST. STATION. N.W.1.

Rickmansworth in 1887, Chesham in 1889 and Aylesbury in 1892.

At Aylesbury, the Met linked to the Aylesbury & Buckingham Railway and began running express trains from Baker Street to Verney Junction, on the Oxford-Bicester-Cambridge route, from 1897.

The Met built subsequent extensions through pastoral acres to Uxbridge in 1904, Watford in 1925 and Stanmore in 1932.

AMERSHAM ON NIGHT TEST RUN

BELOW: a modern view of what would once have been a typical view from deepest Metro-land sees Metropolitan Railway E class 0-4-4T No. 1 standing at Amersham during a night-time test run on May 22, 2013, before a series of specials on the London Underground surface lines for the Met 150 celebrations the following spring bank holiday weekend, as outlined in Chapter 15.

Amersham features in the 1973 BBC TV John Betjeman documentary, Metro-land, about the growth of suburban London in the 20th century. The construction of the railway line was controversial at the time and objections from local landowners prevented its construction until 1892. The station was built a mile to the north of Amersham-on-the-Hill and has provided the focus of this old market town ever since. The line was not electrified until September 12, 1960, when plans made 30 years before finally came to fruition.

The area of the town now known as Amersham-on-the-Hill was referred to as Amersham Common until after the arrival of the railway in 1892, after which the growth of this new area of the town gradually accelerated, with much work being done by the architect John Kennard. It is now known locally as Amersham-on-the-Hill, Amersham town or the 'New Town'. Amersham station is now the northern terminus of the Metropolitan Line. ROBIN JONES

Meanwhile, the line that promoted underground travel in London was now itself becoming heavily involved in residential property development as some of the Met's Metro-land stations were built to serve prospective new developments as opposed to existing ones.

In 1903, the railway laid out a housing estate in Cecil Park, Pinner, to house would-be city dwellers in the countryside, and went on to build others like it, forming its own Country Estates Company in 1919.

The term Metro-land was popularised during the First World War by the English poet, dramatic author and novelist George R Sims as follows:

"I know a land where the wild flowers grow
Near, near at hand if by train you go,
Metro-land, Metro-land."

Suburbia replaced more and more of the sylvan scenes of the Metro-land posters. After the First World War, affordable mortgages brought private housing within the remit of most of London's middle-class and many of its working class people too. Between 1900 and 1930, for example, the population of the Middlesex village of Pinner soared from 3000 to 23,000.

Poet Laureate the late Sir John Betjeman drew much inspiration from Metro- and, praising his virtues in his BBC documentary.

Critics, however, claimed that the Metro-land marketing campaign ruined the countryside permanently, letting it be

HOMES IN METRO-LAND

SEEING IS BELIEVING
NORTH HARROW & PINNER VILLAGE
ROBINSON'S LATEST TYPE
KENTON

WATFORD'S BIGGEST BARGAIN
"COSTIN" HOUSES AT KENTON
CHOOSE A HADDOW HOUSE
EASTBURY PARK, NORTHWOOD

THE CEDARS ESTATE, RICKMANSWORTH
HARROW GARDEN VILLAGE
WELLER ESTATE, AMERSHAM
CANNON CROFT ESTATE, PINNER

PARTICULARS OF TRAIN SERVICE, SEASON TICKET RATES, ETC., OBTAINABLE AT ANY BOOKING OFFICE, OR FROM PUBLICITY MANAGER, 55 BROADWAY, WESTMINSTER, S.W. 1.

METRO-LAND
BRITISH EMPIRE EXHIBITION NUMBER
PRICE THREE-PENCE

ABOVE: The building of the Metropolitan Railway opened up massive new vistas to the west of London for would-be home owners who wanted to escape the city smog and grime. The rural pastures outside the conurbation were marketed as paradise, but soon became urban sprawl. This is a contemporary advertisement for new homes in Metro-land.
LONDON TRANSPORT MUSEUM

ABOVE RIGHT: The guide to Metro-Land published for the British Empire Exhibition of the same year (1924).

conquered by an urban sprawl that could never be rolled back.

After the formation of London Transport in 1935, Metro-land was promoted only as a destination for daytrippers.

By 1936, Met services beyond Aylesbury had ended as the route north of the town was handed over to the national rail network.

The Met became rebranded the Metropolitan Line, and steam trains ran services on its outer sections until 1961. After that, Metropolitan Line services were cut back to Amersham, and so they remain today. Main line services from Marylebone took over the route between Great Missenden and Aylesbury.

In 1988, the Hammersmith & City and East London lines were split off from the Metropolitan line to be run separately.

The Metropolitan Line as we know it today comprises its northern extension from Baker Street to Amersham, Chesham, Uxbridge and Watford through Metro-land. ●

Architect magazine, 1873

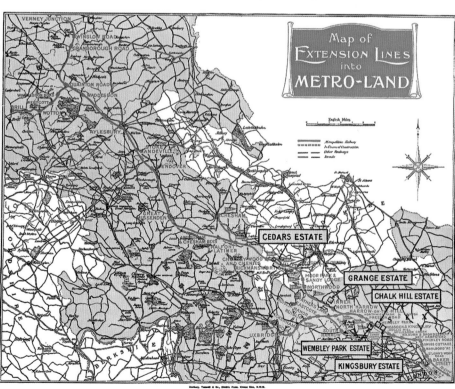

OAKLEIGH PARK
ON MAIN LINE.
DETACHED RESIDENCES
GRAVEL SOIL · OPEN COUNTRY · LARGE PLOTS
MODERATE PRICES.
I. RICH. BUILDER.
EST... OFFICE, CHANDOS AVENUE.

ABOVE: Advertisement for new houses near to the Metropolitan Railway. ROBIN JONES

METRO-LAND
PRICE TWO-PENCE

ABOVE: The Metropolitan Railway's guide to Metro-land, published in 1921.

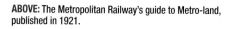

Map of EXTENSION LINES into METRO-LAND

ABOVE: Map of Metro-land, from the 1924 Metro-Land booklet published by the Metropolitan Railway.

Chapter 3

Electrification
of the Met

Widespread electrification of the Underground system began in the early 20th century, but steam locomotives still had a part to play for several decades to come!

ABOVE: No. 1, the first of 10 Metropolitan Railway 1906-built electric locomotives used to haul Aylesbury line trains on the electrified sections in central London and through trains from the Great Western Railway over Inner Circle tracks to Aldgate. LONDON TRANSPORT MUSEUM

The Metropolitan and Metropolitan District railways apart, few steam locomotives were to be found on the lines of other companies that eventually merged under the London Transport umbrella.

While these two companies had introduced the concept of underground lines to London as a means of solving mass transport needs and reducing road congestion, it was the City & South London Railway that would become the world's first deep-level underground tube railway.

The blue clay that lies beneath London is ideal for tunnelling and in 1864 Peter William Barlow patented a circular tunnelling shield and built the Tower Subway, which opened in 1870 using a cable-hauled

railcar, but the rails were removed after only a few months.

Barlow's pupil, James Henry Greathead, made improvements to the design of the shield. In 1883, he promoted a bill to Parliament for the construction of the City of London & Southwark Subway, with himself as engineer.

The City of London and Southwark Subway Act received Royal Assent on July 28, 1884. It allowed for a 'subway' from Short Street at the junction with Newington Butts running to King William Street, consisting of two separate tunnels for traffic in either direction, and accessed by staircases and hydraulic lifts.

In 1886, the year when work started, a further Parliamentary Bill was submitted to extend the tunnels south from Elephant and

Castle to Kennington and Stockwell, and it received assent on July 12, 1887 as the City of London and Southwark Subway (Kennington Extensions) Act 1887.

A third bill led to the City & South London Railway Act 1890 allowing the line to continue south to Clapham Common, and changing the name of the company in the process.

As with the short-lived Tower Subway line, the intention was to use cable haulage, not steam locomotives (expressly prohibited by the original act because of the small size of the tunnels), with the trains attached to the cable by clamps, and the cable wound by a stationary engine.

However, it soon became clear that cable haulage was impractical for a line of the length permitted by the successive Acts of Parliament that had extended the original scheme. A rethink led to the adoption of electric traction, with the power provided by a third rail beneath the train. And so, transport history was made.

In choosing electricity to power the trains, the promoters were building on a legacy of experimentation over the previous decade.

The world's first electric railway appeared in the German town of Lichterfelde in 1881, and two years later, inventor Magnus Volk opened the narrow gauge Volk's Electric Railway on Brighton sea front. The German line is no longer running, so Volk's is the oldest operating electric railway in the world. However, the City & South London became the first major railway in the world to adopt electric traction.

It used small four-wheeled electric locomotives built by Beyer Peacock and Mather & Platt, both of Manchester, and looking every bit like steam trams, collecting a 500v current from the third rail and pulling several carriages.

The railway was opened officially by the future King Edward VII on November 4, 1890, and to the public a fortnight later.

The first services comprised one of the steam tram-like engines hauling three wooden carriages, each of which carried up to 32 passengers, with sliding doors and bench seats running the entire length of each side. Windows were deemed unnecessary and so they quickly became nicknamed 'padded cells' because of their claustrophobic interiors. Despite the cramped conditions, more than five million people rode on the line during 1891, its first full year of operation.

The railway was extended several times north and south; eventually serving 22 stations over 13½ miles from Camden Town in north London to Morden in Surrey, including an extension to Euston, King's Cross and St Pancras, which opened on May, 1907.

In 1913, it became part of the Underground Electric Railways Company of London Limited, in turn becoming part of London Transport 20 years later.

Today the City & South London Railway tunnels and stations form the Bank branch, and the Kennington to Morden section of London Underground's Northern Line.

The second tube line to open in London was the city's shortest. Also designed by Greathead, the Waterloo & City line, which opened on July 11, 1898, runs for just one-and-a-half miles has only two stations, Waterloo and Bank (formerly known as City), but also tunnels beneath the Thames. It is unique among London's underground lines in that it's subterranean for its entire length. Also, it is not connected to any other railway.

Following the success of the City & South London Railway and the Waterloo & City Railway, the deep-level Central London Railway, now the Central Line, which was authorised to run from Shepherd's Bush to Bank, was opened on June 27, 1900.

The route is the longest on the Underground, with 20 of its 49 stations beneath the surface.

These three kick-started the building of tube lines beneath London and used electric traction apart from steam, and a full history of

ABOVE: The changeover from steam to electric traction on the Metropolitan Railway began in 1905 and lasted until 1961. Metropolitan line steam and electric locomotives stand side by side in the early Twenties: the electric one with an Aylesbury destination board is No. 19. LONDON TRANSPORT MUSEUM

ABOVE: The trial trip of the first Metropolitan Railway electric train on December 13, 1904. The press was also invited and The Times reported the next day: "(we are) celebrating the beginning of a new era in the history of the old underground railways from which smoke, dirt and discomfort will be nearly banished." The public service started on January 1, 1905 between Baker Street and Uxbridge. The primary purpose of electrification was to exclude steam locomotives from the tunnels of the inner London area. The steam locomotives' drivers and firemen were retrained as motormen. The view shows the rear of the train and various members of Metropolitan Railway staff. LONDON TRANSPORT MUSEUM

the growth of today's Underground network is beyond the remit of this book.

However, it is worth recalling the history of the Piccadilly Line, if only because of the origin of the term 'underground'.

The Piccadilly Line was originally known as the Great Northern, Piccadilly & Brompton Railway. It was one of several railways controlled by the Underground Electric Railways Co of London Ltd, a holding company owned by Charles Tyson Yerkes, who had helped develop an extensive urban transit system in Chicago and intended to create a similar empire in London.

By 1902, Yerkes had bought the cash-strapped Metropolitan District Railway, now the District Line, and built the Charing Cross, Euston & Hampstead Railway, the Baker Street & Waterloo Railway and the Great Northern, Piccadilly & Brompton Railway.

This group was referred to as the 'Yerkes tube', but the lines were not one company at the outset. In 1908, they adopted joint branding as the 'Underground'.

Yerkes died in New York aged 68 in 1905, before he could see any of his works on the London railways completed.

To promote travel by the underground railways, in London a joint marketing arrangement was agreed. In 1908, the Met joined this scheme, which included maps, joint publicity and through ticketing. Underground signs were used outside stations in Central London.

From 1905, the Metropolitan Railway, the predecessor of all the underground lines, both in the UK and worldwide, was electrified in stages as it expanded.

At the start of the 20th century, the Met and the District saw increased competition in central London from the new electric deep-level tube lines.

With the opening in 1900 of the Central London Railway with a flat fare of 2d, the pair together lost four million passengers in a year from the second half of 1899.

The polluted atmosphere in the tunnels was becoming increasingly unpopular with ▶

ABOVE: City & South London Railway electric locomotive No. 13, built by Mather & Platt in 1890, on display at London Transport Museum in Covent Garden. ROBIN JONES

ABOVE: Metropolitan Railway Bo-Bo electric No. 5 *John Hampden* preserved inside London Transport Museum. ROBIN JONES

passengers and conversion to electric traction was seen as the way forward.

Electrification had been considered by the Met as early as the 1880s, but such a method of traction was still in its infancy, and agreement would be needed with the District because of the shared ownership of the Inner Circle.

A jointly owned train of six coaches ran an experimental passenger service on the Earls Court to High Street Kensington section for six months in 1900. It was deemed a success, and in 1901 a Met and District joint committee recommended the Ganz three-phase AC system with overhead wires.

This arrangement was accepted by both parties until Yerkes' Underground Electric Railways Company of London took control of the District. Yerkes favoured DC with a third rail similar to that on the City & South London and Central London railways. Following arbitration by the Board of Trade a DC system with four rails was taken up and the railways began electrifying using multiple-unit stock and electric locomotives hauling carriages.

The Met opened a 10.5MW coal-fired power station in 1904 at Neasden, which supplied 11kV 33.3 Hz current to five substations that converted this to 600v DC using rotary converters.

The District, meanwhile, had been building a line from Ealing to South Harrow and had authority for an extension to Uxbridge. When, in 1899, the District had problems raising the finance, the Met came to the rescue with a package whereby it would build a branch from Harrow to Rayners Lane and take over the line to Uxbridge, with the District retaining running rights for up to three trains an hour.

The necessary act was passed in 1899 and the building of the 7½-mile branch started in September 1902. As this line was under construction it was included in the list of lines to be electrified, together with the railway from Baker Street to Harrow, the Inner Circle and the joint GWR and Met Hammersmith & City.

The Met opened the line to Uxbridge on June 30, 1904 with one intermediate station at Ruislip, initially worked by steam. Wooden platforms the length of three cars opened at Ickenham on September 25, 1905, followed by similar simple structures at Eastcote and Rayners Lane on May 26, 1906.

Electric multiple units began running on January 1, 1905, By March 20 all local services between Baker Street and Harrow were electric.

The use of six-car trains was considered wasteful on the lightly used line to Uxbridge and in running an off-peak three-car shuttle to Harrow the Met annoyed the Board of Trade by using a motor car to propel two trailers. A short steam train was used for off-peak services from the end of March while some trailers were modified to add a driving cab, entering service from June 1.

On July 1, 1905, the Met and the District both introduced electric units on the Inner Circle, however, later that day a Met multiple unit overturned the positive current rail on the District and the Met service was withdrawn. An incompatibility was found between the way the shoe-gear was mounted on Met trains, and so the District track and Met trains were withdrawn from the District and modified.

Nevertheless, full electric services started on September 24, reducing the travel time around the Circle from 70 to 50 minutes.

ABOVE: A six-car train of new Metropolitan Railway electric stock, seen at Neasden depot in 1905. LONDON TRANSPORT MUSEUM

The GWR built a 6MW power station at Park Royal and electrified the line between Paddington and Hammersmith as well as the branch from Latimer Road to Kensington (Addison Road). An electric service with jointly owned rolling stock started on the Hammersmith & City on November 5, 1906. That same year, the Met suspended running on the East London Railway, terminating instead at the District station at Whitechapel until that line was electrified in 1913.

The Met line beyond Harrow-on-the-Hill was not electrified so trains were hauled by an electric locomotive from Baker Street and changed for a steam locomotive en route. From January 1, 1907, the exchange took place at Wembley Park, and from July 19, 1908, locomotives were changed at Harrow.

GWR rush-hour services over the Met and Hammersmith & City continued to operate, electric traction taking over from steam at Paddington from January 1907, although freight services to Smithfield continued to be steam-hauled throughout.

Following electrification, the outer suburban routes were worked with carriage stock hauled from Baker Street by an electric locomotive that was exchanged for a steam locomotive en route.

The Met ordered 20 electric locomotives from Metropolitan Amalgamated with two types of electrical equipment. The first 10, with Westinghouse equipment, entered service in 1906. These 'camel-back' bogie locomotives had a central cab, weighed 50 tons and had four 215hp (160kW) traction motors.

The second type was built to a boxcar design with British Thomson-Houston equipment, which replaced the Westinghouse type in 1919.

In the early Twenties, the Met contracted Metropolitan-Vickers of Barrow-in-Furness to rebuild these 20 locomotives. However, when work started on the first locomotive, it was found to be impractical and uneconomical and the order was changed to building new locomotives using some of the equipment recovered from the originals.

The new locomotives were built in 1922-23 and named after famous London residents.

They had four 300hp (220kW) motors, totalling 1200hp (880kW), giving a top speed of 65mph.

Two of these Bo-Bo electrics are preserved, No. 5 *John Hampden* in the London Transport Museum in Covent Garden and No. 12 *Sarah Siddons*, which is still operational and used for heritage events, as highlighted in Chapter 10 and thereafter.

The first order for electric multiple units was placed with Metropolitan Amalgamated in 1902 for 50 trailers and 20 motor cars with Westinghouse equipment, which ran as six-car trains. First- and third-class accommodation was provided in open saloons, second class being withdrawn from the Met.

Access was at the ends via open lattice gates, and the units were modified so that they could run off-peak as three-car units.

For the joint Hammersmith & City service, the Met and the GWR bought 20 six-car trains. In 1904, a further order was placed by the Met for 36 motor cars and 62 trailers

with an option for another 20 motor cars and 40 trailers.

From 1906, some of the Ashbury bogie stock hitherto hauled by steam locomotives was converted into multiple units by fitting cabs, control equipment and motors. In 1910, two motor cars were modified with driving cabs at both ends. They started work on the Uxbridge-South Harrow shuttle service, being transferred to the Addison Road shuttle in 1918. From 1925 to 1934 these vehicles were used between Watford and Rickmansworth.

In 1913, an order was placed for 23 motor cars and 20 trailers for use on the Circle. They were followed in 1921 by 20 motor cars, 33 trailers and six first-class driving trailers.

Between 1927 and 1933 both the Metropolitan Carriage & Wagon and Birmingham Railway Carriage & Wagon companies built multiple-unit compartment stock for the Met for services from Baker Street and the City to Watford and Rickmansworth. ●

ABOVE: The interior of a City & South London Railway 'padded cell' carriage No. 30 as exhibited in London Transport Museum at Covent Garden. No windows were provided as the railway took the view that there was nothing to see in the tunnels! ROBIN JONES

LEFT: One of the Metropolitan Railway's Metropolitan Vickers Bo-Bo electrics was displayed at the 1925 British Empire Exhibition at Wembley, with its side panel removed to show the circuitry. LONDON TRANSPORT MUSEUM

Chapter 4

The branch
where time stood still

London Transport developed an electrified system that was the envy of the world, with electrified railways both below and above ground providing a fast and efficient rapid transit system. However, the remotest outpost of the London Underground system was a world, if not a universe, apart. In rural Buckinghamshire, far, far from any madding crowd, the Underground briefly operated an eccentric six-and-a-half mile branch that looked every bit as if it was from the dawn of the steam era.

Back in the mid-Thirties, the Buckinghamshire village of Brill was the furthest point that you could travel from the capital via London Underground. However, few people ever did.

Fifty-one miles from the Baker Street terminus of the Metropolitan Line, passengers who travelled this far found no sleek tube trains whizzing through tunnels.

Instead, there were Metropolitan Railway steam locomotives heading rakes of vintage wooden carriages back and forth from the junction with the main line at Quainton Road, a route shared by the Met and the Great Central Railway.

Before they came, the branch from Quainton Road to Brill had used flywheel-driven locomotives that looked every bit like traction engines.

This little branch was built by the third Duke of Buckingham and Chandos, who lived at early 18th-century Wotton House, and who was chairman of the London & North Western Railway from 1853-61.

Initially titled the Wotton Tramway because of the estate it served, and later known as the Brill Tramway, the Duke had it built on his land for agricultural and industrial use between 1870-72.

It was also opened as a public railway. The first section from Quainton Road to Wotton came into use on April 1, 1871, and the whole line to Brill was completed by the summer of the following year.

Running from Quainton Road (opened by the Aylesbury & Buckingham Railway in 1868) to Waddesdon (renamed Waddesdon Road in 1922 to distinguish it from Waddesdon Manor on the main line between Aylesbury and Quainton Road), Westcott, Wotton and Wood Siding, its western terminus beneath the hilltop village of Brill was 700ft above sea level.

Initially there was a halt at Church Siding, between Wotton and Wood Siding, at the junction with a spur to Woodham near Kingswood, the site of a coal wharf. A branch line connected the tramway to a brick and tile works.

During the first few months of operation, the tramway was operated by horses, and between 1872 and 1906, by its own steam locomotives.

BELOW: The Brill Tramway was recreated at the Buckinghamshire Railway Centre on October 9, 2005. Visiting 1895-built Aveling & Porter flywheel-driven locomotive *Sydenham*, similar to the line's first two engines, hauled the centre's replica Brill Tramway coach. PHIL BARNES

ABOVE: One of two Aveling & Porter locomotives supplied to the Wotton, later Brill, Tramway in 1872, and now in the ownership of London Transport Museum. It is pictured on display at the Buckinghamshire Railway Centre. ROBIN JONES

The first two locomotives were very unconventional 0-4-0 single-cylinder geared steam locomotives supplied by Aveling & Porter, works numbers 807 and 846, supplied at a cost of £400 each. Each 10-ton locomotive had a single over-slung cylinder connected through a countershaft and pinion to further pinions on the axles. Their maximum speed was about 8mph.

Both were later sold to Nether Heyford brickworks, near Weedon in Northamptonshire, which kept them until 1950. No. 807 as No.1 survives in the ownership of London Transport Museum and is currently on loan to *Buckinghamshire Railway Centre*.

The next two locomotives were supplied by WG Bagnall of Stoke-on-Trent, in the form of 0-4-0 saddle tank *Buckingham*, works number 16 of 1876, and 0-4-0 tank engine *Wootton*, number 120 of 1877. They had 'reversed' inside cylinders to drive the front axle.

The operation of the tramway was at first contracted out, while maintenance work was undertaken by the Duke's own staff.

Signalling was a primitive affair, but only one engine was in use on the tramway at any one time.

The operating regulations were notably strict: a rule book published in 1873 listed fines, which might be levied on staff for misdemeanours, such as: "If the train be late at Quainton Junction in consequence of a late start, the fault of the driver in not having his engine ready, a fine of half a day's pay to be imposed."

A scheme to build an Oxford, Aylesbury & Metropolitan Junction Railway by extending the tramway from Brill to the great university city 10 miles away, was drawn up in 1883, but nothing ever came of it.

In 1888, Parliament approved a similar scheme drawn up by the Oxford & Aylesbury Tramway Company, which took over the running of the Brill Tramway in 1894 on the death of the Duke. Its Oxford terminus would have been near Magdalen Bridge on the edge of the city centre. However, the necessary ▶

ABOVE: An early picture of one of the tramway's first locomotives. LONDON TRANSPORT MUSEUM

ABOVE: An Aveling & Porter steam engine hauling a passenger train on the Brill Tramway around 1890.
LONDON TRANSPORT MUSEUM

money could not be raised and the cost of tunnelling beneath 600ft Muswell Hill to the west of Brill would probably have proved too expensive.

Nevertheless, the Oxford & Aylesbury Tramroad Company improved the tramway, replacing the original light rails laid on longitudinal sleepers with flat-bottomed rails spiked directly to transverse sleepers as well as much of the rolling stock.

Out went the Aveling & Porters, and in came Manning Wardle industrial-type 0-6-0 saddle tanks with inside cylinders, one being replaced by another Manning Wardle in 1899. They were *Earl Temple*, works number 1249 of 1894; *Huddersfield*, works number 616; a

second-hand locomotive built 1876, withdrawn in 1899, and Wotton No. 2, works number 1415, built in 1899. *Earl Temple* was later renamed Brill No 1.

In December 1899, the Metropolitan Railway, which built the first physical link between the tramway and the main line, acquired a lease on it, and brought in new locomotives and rolling stock, but never exercised an option to buy it outright. That was hardly surprising in view of the low anticipated returns.

Poet Laureate the late Sir John Betjeman would later recall fond memories of the tramway during a visit to Quainton Road in 1929. In his 1973 television

documentary Metroland, he spoke of watching the Brill branch train depart, "the steam ready to take two or three passengers through oil-lit halts and over level crossings, a rather bumpy journey."

When the London Passenger Transport Board was formed, taking over all the underground railway companies, it also reluctantly inherited the Brill Tramway.

The mid-Thirties saw closures of many famous light railways as motor transport rendered them financially unviable, including the Leek & Manifold Valley, the Lynton & Barnstaple and the Welsh Highland.

The Brill Tramway was no exception and on November 30, 1935, the board closed it, along with all stations beyond Aylesbury.

Nothing remains of the tramway today, apart from privately owned Westcott station, but its route can be seen in a double row of hedges running parallel to the lane to the west of Quainton Road.

Passenger trains on the Great Central route from Marylebone to Nottingham ceased to call at Quainton Road from 1963, and on September 3, 1966, the complete route was closed to passengers apart from services between Nottingham and Rugby, which lingered on until 1969.

Quainton Road station is now home to the Quainton Railway Society's Buckinghamshire Railway Centre. The wooden waiting room on platforms 2 and 3 at the station was once the shelter for passengers waiting for Brill branch trains.

In recent years, two Aveling & Porter locomotives, similar to those used on the tramway, have been based at the centre at one time or another.

In the early 21st century, members built a replica Brill Tramway coach to offer the public rides behind one of them.

BELOW: Metropolitan Railway A class 4-4-0 No. 23 of 1866 stands at Wood Siding station on the Brill branch on September 21, 1934, when the tramway was part of the London Underground empire.
LONDON TRANSPORT MUSEUM

ABOVE: Metropolitan Railway Manning Wardle locomotive Brill No. 2 running on the Brill branch around 1900. LONDON TRANSPORT MUSEUM

ABOVE RIGHT: A printed 1870s freight tariff for the Wotton Tramway, with prices for the carriage of various types of material, delivery days and train times and other conditions. LONDON TRANSPORT MUSEUM

RIGHT: End of the line: Brill station as pictured in 1935, its final year of operation. LONDON TRANSPORT MUSEUM

At one stage, some members drew up plans to relay at least part of the Brill Tramway, running a mile from Quainton Road.

However, these plans were finally scuppered by the publication of the Government's plans for HS2, which is pencilled in immediately to the west of the centre, cutting straight through the tramway formation. ●

AYLESBURY & BUCKINGHAM RAILWAY, AND WOTTON TRAMWAY.

Arrangements have been made by which **GOODS** and **PARCELS** can be Booked through, between AYLESBURY and the undermentioned Places in **WOTTON TRAMWAY** District, on and after 1st December next, (including collection or delivery,) at the following Rates. viz.—

Ale and Porter	6d.	per Cwt.
Groceries, in Mixed Packages	6d.	"
Hardware	6d.	"
Haberdashery and General Drapery	7½d.	"
Earthenware, in Casks and Crates	6d.	"
Leather	6d.	"
Iron and General Ironmongery	6d.	"
Wines and Spirits, in Casks and Cases	6d.	"
Ditto, in Hampers	7½d.	"
Ditto, in Jars or Bottles (protected by basketwork)	7½d.	"
Ditto (protected by basketwork) if in over 4-gall. size	9d.	"
	Under 14lbs.	Above 14lbs. and until more by weight.
Single Parcels or Packages	6d. each.	8d. each.

DELIVERIES MADE AS FOLLOWS:

Brill and Wotton	Daily.
Boarstall, Oakley, & Little London	Wednesdays & Saturdays.
Ham Green, Kingswood, Grendon, and Edgcott	Tuesdays, Wednesdays, Fridays, and Saturdays.
Dorton, Ashendon, and Pollicott	Wednesdays & Saturdays.
Ludgershall and Piddington	Mondays and Thursdays.

☞ Any further particulars can be obtained at the Offices of the Aylesbury and Buckingham Railway, Aylesbury; or any of the Offices on the Wotton Tramway.

Aylesbury, 12th November, 1872.

DE FRAINE, PRINTER, "BUCKS HERALD" OFFICES, AYLESBURY.

COUNTRY JOYS ON LONDON'S UNDERGROUND

ABOVE: One of the Brill Tramway coaches ended its days as a platform waiting room. LONDON TRANSPORT MUSEUM

LEFT: London Underground is best known for its tunnels beneath the capital, but in the early 20th century made much of its potential for day trips to the countryside, to outposts such as Quainton Road and Brill.

Chapter 5

The maroon panniers:
Last steam on the Underground... for now

Possibly remembered best of all of the steam locomotives that ran on London Underground were the 13 Great Western railway 57XX pannier tanks, which were bought second-hand from British Railways, and repainted into an attractive lined maroon livery, which some are carrying once again.

The steel wheels of steam turned full circle on the London Underground. As we saw in Chapter 1, the first locomotives used on the initial stage of the Metropolitan Railway were supplied by the GWR.

The last steam engines to run over the system were also GWR locomotives, in the form of 13 57XX pannier tanks.

In late 1953, London Underground looked at replacing its steam fleet with British Railways' 350hp diesel shunters, as the boilers of the Metropolitan Railway locomotives were wearing out.

A Great Northern Railway J52 0-6-0 saddle tank, No. 68862, was borrowed from British Railways Eastern Region, but failed to impress, having a leaking tank and safety valve.

Attention then turned to GWR pannier tanks. Several 57XXs based at Old Oak Common had worked engineers' trains during the project to extend the Central Line from North Acton to West Ruislip after the Second World War, and had been reliable, efficient and versatile.

Totalling 863 examples built between 1929 and 1950, the 57XX panniers comprised the second-biggest steam locomotive class in British railway history, and could readily handle passenger, freight or shunting duties.

They were produced during the reign of GWR Chief Mechanical Engineer, Charles Collett, who was not a great inventor like his predecessor George Jackson Churchward, but a marvellous innovator, who would adapt designs from past decades by upgrading them in line with modern technology.

His 57XX design was largely based on the 2721 class of 0-6-0 saddle tanks, built at Swindon Works between 1897-1901.

The first 57XXs appeared in January 1929 and building continued almost non-stop until December 1950. The first batch, Nos. 5700-49, was not built at Swindon, but by the North British Locomotive Company in Glasgow.

The first Swindon batch, built to Lot 258, were numbered 5750-79, and appeared in 1929, The second Swindon batch, built to Lot 260, were numbered 5750-99 and built during 1929-30.

They were found right across the GWR system, hauling empty coaching stock in and out of Paddington, heading rural branch line services and marshalling coal trains in the South Wales coalfield. After Nationalisation, several 57XXs found their way to other regions of British Railways, giving sterling service until dieselisation.

By the mid-Fifties, some examples were becoming surplus to Western Region requirements, and to Underground officials, seemed a far better bet than a type such as the J52, which had its origins in the 1880s.

In 1956, the Western Region agreed to a London Transport request to try out a 57XX. Accordingly, No. 7711 was despatched from Old Oak Common to Swindon Works for repairs before being sent to the Underground's Lillie Bridge depot on February 27.

TIGHT FIT

Modifications were found to be necessary after trials between Finchley Road and Baker Street showed that the clearance was found to be very tight, with little more than two inches between the pannier's rain gutter and the tunnel wall.

In May that year, London Transport elected to use 57XXs as the standard locomotive on engineering trains.

London Transport paid £3160 for No. 7711, and at the same time decided to buy a second one, No. 5752, which became L91 in May 1957, after it was modified and painted in maroon livery for Underground traffic. The panniers were also for the first time fitted with curtains in the cabs to keep out the smoke and fumes when in the tunnels.

The Underground agreed to buy a pannier a year to replace the existing steam locomotives such as the remaining E class members.

The next two panniers to arrive on the Underground were Nos. 5786 (L92) and No. 7779 (L93), in 1958, followed by No. 7752 (L94) in 1959.

In 1960, L91 was despatched to Swindon Works for boiler and firebox repairs. An examination revealed that it would be cheaper to provide London Transport with a recently withdrawn replacement pannier than to carry out the job.

As such, No. 5757 became the second L91, instead of L96 as scheduled, and the original L91 was scrapped.

Similarly, in 1961 L90 was sent back to Swindon and replaced with No. 7760, which became the new L90, instead of L95.

No. 5764 arrived in 1960 to become L9, No. 7741 was bought in 1961 and became L96, and in 1962, No. 7749 (L97) and No. 7739 (L98) joined the fleet.

The last pair No. 5775 (L89) and No. 7715 (L99) were delivered in 1963, the year that the Metropolitan Railway marked its centenary. This pair made up the last of the 13 maroon LT panniers.

In Underground service, the panniers were primarily used for freight trips taking material and plans between Lillie Bridge and Acton depots, as well as shunting there, and hauling rubbish trains from Neasden to Croxley Tip near Watford. ▶

ABOVE: A driver's eye view of Neasden depot on July 1, 1970 from the footplate of LT pannier L90. Battery locomotive No. 22 stands on the adjacent track, while trains of Underground A stock and 1938 tube stock are in the sidings. DR HEINZ ZINRAM/ TFL, LONDON TRANSPORT MUSEUM

ABOVE: Underground pannier L90 shunting at Neasden depot on May 27, 1970. A rake of open wagons is coupled behind the locomotive, with a brake van at the rear. DR HEINZ ZINRAM/ LONDON TRANSPORT MUSEUM

ABOVE: A typical plank wagon, which would have been included in a freight or engineer's train on the Underground, preserved at Buckinghamshire Railway Centre. ROBIN JONES

RIGHT: GWR pannier tanks could also be seen on the Underground's Paddington station as well as the main line terminus. L95 is seen heading a goods train on May 24, 1969. FRANK DUMBLETON

BELOW: GWR 57XX pannier tank No. 776 in London Transport livery as L90, was one of the last three steam locomotives used by London Underground. LONDON TRANSPORT MUSEUM

THE CLOCK TICKING...

Several other panniers were sold into industry by the Western Region, mainly for working colliery systems in South Wales.

Those on the Underground may have escaped the scrapyard for the moment, but were living on borrowed time.

Swindon Works informed London Transport that it could guarantee steam repair facilities only until 1967, following the demise of steam on the Western Region.

In 1963, plans were being drawn up to replace the panniers either with diesels or new battery-electric locomotives.

When, in March 1966, the last heavy general overhaul of a British Railways' pannier tank was carried out at Eastleigh Works on the Southern Region, London Transport decided that any of its steam engines needing a major overhaul would have to be scrapped, as from then on no repair facilities were available.

In 1966, L96 was withdrawn, with the second L91 and L93 following the next year. In 1968, Nos. L97 and L98 were taken out of traffic. L92 followed in 1969, and was preserved, along with the others that remained in service at that point.

In 1970, it was decided to buy second-hand Rolls Royce-engined Sentinel 0-6-0 diesel-hydraulic shunters to take over from the panniers.

Pannier Nos. L89 and L99 were withdrawn in 1970, leaving just three in service.

By this time, the railway preservation movement had evolved to the point where several heritage lines were eager to buy them.

ABOVE: L90 working an engineer's train near Watford in the dying years of London Underground steam. LONDON TRANSPORT MUSEUM

ABOVE: The end is nigh: L95 (5764) at Watford Tip sidings in its final months on the Underground. LONDON TRANSPORT MUSEUM

ABOVE: Sadly, only six out of 13 London Transport 57XXs found a new home on preservation railways. L98, (7739) awaiting the cutter's torch in the yard of Chesterfield Steelbreaking & Dismantling Ltd, Derbyshire, along with the remains of an unknown member of the same class, in February 1970. PETE HACKNEY*

ABOVE: London Transport pannier L98 (GWR 7739) hauls a cable-laying train. LONDON TRANSPORT MUSEUM

ABOVE: Unloved and barely cared for, with its London Transport paintwork peeling. L95 is seen shunting at Croxley tip in June 1969. 8474TIM*

ABOVE: Poster advertising the last steam on the Underground on June 6, 1971. LONDON TRANSPORT MUSEUM **ABOVE RIGHT:** Flyer for the special 'last steam' open day at Neasden depot. LONDON TRANSPORT MUSEUM

THE END OF AN ERA

The last three London Transport panniers were the final steam locomotives in service on a UK main line. The narrow gauge Vale of Rheidol Railway and steam cranes apart, British Railways ended the use of steam haulage on August 11, 1968. The 'Fifteen Guinea Special' from Liverpool via Manchester to Carlisle and back brought down the curtain on 164 years of history since the railway locomotive was first demonstrated in public on the Penydarren Tramroad near Merthyr Tydfil by Cornishman Richard Trevithick. The final pre-preservation main line steam-hauled passenger trains anywhere the British Isles ran between Belfast and Whitehead on Easter Tuesday 1970.

The pannier-hauled stores trains for Acton Works ended in February 1971 and then battery locomotives took over the Watford Tip runs.

The final 'real' revenue-earning run by a London Transport pannier was a freight working between Lillie Bridge and Neasden on June 4. L90 headed the train, but broke down and it had to be rescued by a battery locomotive.

Acknowledging the huge public interest, London Transport announced a final day of steam operation on the Underground, on Sunday, June 6, 1971; it attracted huge public interest.

Requests for a steam-hauled passenger train were turned down, However, it was agreed to run a demonstration engineer's train so that a red pannier in action could be photographed and glimpsed for one last time.

Special travel cards with a pannier tank logo were printed, allowing travel on the day and

ABOVE: Still carrying London Transport maroon livery, L95 (GWR 5764) moves into Bridgnorth station yard on the Severn Valley Railway on August 8, 1971. It featured in the 1961 Railway Roundabout TV series in a feature about London Underground steam. RAY O'HARA

also entry to a rolling stock exhibition held at Neasden shed.

Crowds packed all the Underground platforms along the route to be taken by the train, from Moorgate to Farringdon and Neasden, after it had travelled from Neasden to the starting point.

Headed by L94, at Farringdon the train switched from the Widened Lines to the Circle Line and ran via Baker Street and the Metropolitan Line to Finchley Road where it stopped for a short time.

The train then changed over to the Bakerloo Line and at 3pm entered Neasden, which was packed with 8500 visitors, around 2000 of whom had arrived by Underground specials. On display in the depot were the replacement Sentinel diesels.

A THIRD LEASE OF LIFE

Six of the former Underground panniers found a third lease of life on heritage railways. No. 5764, which was built at Swindon in June 1929 and became L95, was sold directly out ▶

BELOW: Reliveried as L92, GWR 0-6-0PT No. 5786, which began its heritage-era career at the Severn Valley Railway, made a return visit to celebrate the line's 50th anniversary by starring in the March 20-22, 2015 spring steam gala. It is seen rounding the curve by the West Midlands Safari Park towards Foley Park tunnel. ALAN WEAVER

of service to the Severn Valley Railway after the line's Kidderminster branch set up a fund to acquire one of the three last panniers in London Transport service.

L95 was steamed on June 19, 1971, the day it arrived at Bridgnorth, being lit up before it had been removed from the low-loader on which it was delivered. Used in London Transport maroon livery during its first season on the Severn Valley, it was restored to GWR Brunswick green in 1972.

As No. 5764, it appeared several times in the 1976 BBC TV adaptation of Charles Dickens' short ghost story The Signalman.

It was withdrawn from traffic on December 31, 2010, and at the time of writing is displayed in the Severn Valley's Engine House museum and visitor centre at Highley awaiting overhaul.

Also taken to the Severn Valley Railway from the capital was L92 (5786) after it was withdrawn from traffic on October 3, 1969, and sold for £1100 in full working order to the Worcester Locomotive Society.

No. 5786 was taken by lorry to Bridgnorth from where it was steamed to Bewdley and restored to GWR livery.

In May 1970 the locomotive travelled in steam to Tyseley for a festival of transport. While it returned to Bridgnorth, it never worked on the Severn Valley again.

It was transferred to the former Bulmer Railway Centre at Hereford, a heritage railway venue set up by cidermaker HP Bulmer, and used on short passenger trips.

The centre was closed in 1993 to make way for more space at the cider plant, and the owning group took it to the South Devon Railway, where the pannier has been based ever since.

Following its latest overhaul, it returned in March 2013, wearing London Transport maroon livery as L92 once again, to mark 150th anniversary of the opening of the first section of London Underground in 1863.

ABOVE: London Transport pannier L92 was delivered by road to the Severn Valley Railway on October 4, 1969. SVR ARCHIVES

BELOW: GWR pannier tank No. 5764, which carried the number L95 in London Transport service, pulls into Bewdley with a three-coach service train en route to Kidderminster, back in its Brunswick green livery. The trend in recent years has been for owners of some of the ex-London Transport panniers to repaint them into the eye-catching maroon livery in which they worked on the Underground. BRIAN SHARPE

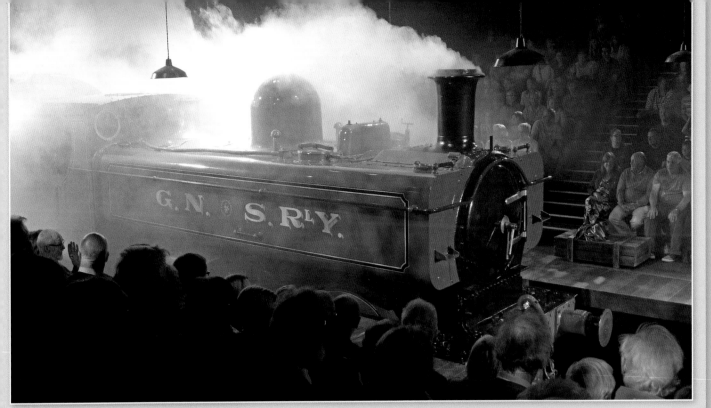

IMMORTALISED ON THE BIG SCREEN

International fame lay in store for L89 (5775), when it was sold to the Keighley & Worth Valley Railway as one of its earliest duties in traffic was to take a starring role in EMI's big-screen adaptation of Edith A Nesbit's classic novel The Railway Children.

Painted in ochre for the fictional Great Northern & Southern Railway, it was coupled to the 'Old Gentleman's Saloon' – the film went on to become a worldwide smash hit.

Why let historical accuracy get in the way of a good fantasy? As a novel, The Railway Children was published in 1906, 23 years before the first 57XX appeared. Yet the cinema-going public loved it, and not only did the film place the KWVR firmly on the tourist map, but did much to boost the profile of the operational heritage railway movement as a whole, at a time when it was struggling to raise a head of steam.

A total of 39 days of location filming took place on the line in 1970, with No. 5775 taking a starring role alongside the likes of Jenny Agutter, Dinah Sheridan, Sally Thomsett, Bernard Cribbins and William Mervyn.

The conclusion of the film is the famous, "Daddy, my daddy!" scene where the children's father, having been freed from wrongful imprisonment, emerges at the station through a cloud of steam to be greeted by his eldest daughter, played by Jenny Agutter.

For the filming, Manchester Ship Canal Hudswell Clarke 0-6-0T No. 67 had been booked, having been fitted with a continuous steam pipe, which ran beneath the floorboards of the coaches behind, so it could emit a cloud of steam across the platform. However, the wrong train was sent, hauled by pannier L89, with the Old Gentleman's Saloon, minus any steam pipe or means of producing the cloud.

A special-effects man tried to save the day by attaching a long rubber hose to one of the pannier's injector overflow pipes and running it beneath the train. It did produce a cloud of steam as required over the platform, until the injector overheated and a joint burst.

Jeffries, the director, took the blunder in his stride, and arranged for the correct train to be brought the following day.

For four decades, people have visited the KWVR to see the line where the film was made. For many years they travelled behind the pannier in its 'movie' livery, before it was repainted back into London Transport maroon.

The pannier reprised its film role in the summer of 2015. After some years as a static exhibit in the locomotive shed at Oxenhope waiting for its next overhaul, it was taken to Locomotion: The National Railway Museum at Shildon, and repainted into the livery it carried in the film.

It was then taken to York, where it became the star of the latest stage production of The Railway Children at the National Railway Museum, a joint venture with York Theatre Royal, and for which a special temporary venue, The Signal Box Theatre, was erected in the south yard. ▶

RIGHT: L89 (No. 5775), in its Great Northern & Southern Railway 'movie' livery, heads a service train on the Keighley & Worth Valley Railway. The international success of this film not only helped place this railway on the tourist map but gave a fillip to the heritage railway movement when it was still in its early stages. BRIAN SHARPE BELOW: Pannier L89 (5775) is brought to a halt by the petticoat-waving children who prevented a rail disaster in the EMI smash hit version of The Railway Children in 1970. KWVR

TWO FOR TYSELEY

ABOVE: London Transport maroon livery back on the main line: pannier L94 raises a head of steam as it double-heads with sister No. 9600 through Hinckley with a Vintage Trains' main line special from Tyseley on November 3, 2010. BRIAN SHARPE

The last steam engine on a British mainland main line, L94 (7752) was bought straight out of service by 7029 Clun Castle Ltd, the owning group of the Tyseley Collection of locomotives, which formed the basis of Birmingham Railway Museum.

It appeared at the June 1971 Tyseley open day in London Transport maroon and was afterwards repainted into GWR livery.

Over the past four decades it has visited several heritage railways and also been approved for main line running. To mark the 40th anniversary of its final run on the Underground, in 2011 it was returned to London Transport livery as L94.

The 'second' L90, (7760) was also bought by 7029 Clun Castle Ltd and arrived in June 1971, after initially being sold to the

Steelbreaking and Dismantling Company of Sheffield, which had cut up sisters Nos. 7741 (L96) and 7779 (L93) in autumn 1968, and Nos. 7739 (L98) and 7749 (L97) in January 1970.

No. 7760 did not officially enter service at Tyseley until the late 1980s, and visited other heritage lines, also gaining main line certification.

On October 14, 2001, No. 7760 was used as a banking engine on the famous Lickey Incline, at 1-in-37.7 the steepest sustained main line railway gradient in Britain. The engine helped Tyseley shedmates GWR 4-6-0s 4965 *Rood Ashton Hall* and then 4936 *Kinlet Hall* up the incline.

ABOVE: Resplendent in maroon livery, L94 stands on the turntable at Tyseley Locomotive Works during the June 25, 2011 open day. ROBIN JONES

ABOVE: The last maroon pannier on the Underground: this miniature live steam model of L99 was displayed at London Transport Museum's Acton Depot open weekend on April 13-14, 2013, held as one of several events to mark the 150th anniversary of the Metropolitan Railway. ROBIN JONES

ABOVE: L94 (7752) gives passenger rides during a Tyseley Locomotive Works open day. PHIL PARKER*

With Tyseley owning two other panniers certified for main line running, No. 7760 is out of its boiler ticket. Tyseley has indicated that it may be willing to sell it if a good home at another heritage location can be found.

L99 (7715) was withdrawn on New Year's Day 1970 and bought by the London Railway Preservation Society, which had turned Quainton Road station into what is now the Buckinghamshire Railway Centre. It reached there the following day.

Steamed at the centre's Easter open days that year, it was then taken out of traffic for overhaul.

Back in service at Easter 1972, it reappeared with its original GWR numberplates as No. 771.

It underwent a heavy overhaul in 1979, and was later upgraded to British Rail main line standard so that, as L99 once more, it could work special steam trains on the London Underground from Neasden depot, during the popular former Steam on the Met events, as described in Chapter 8.

Later also repainted into London Transport livery, in March 2011, as L99, it began a two-year loan to the North Norfolk Railway, but was later withdrawn with a cracked boiler foundation ring. ●

ABOVE: The National Railway Museum's Railfest 2012 event at York saw Tyseley's London Transport-liveried pannier L94 (GWR 7752) line up alongside Metropolitan Railway electric locomotive No. 12 *Sarah Siddons*. ANDREW COWELL

THE 13 LONDON TRANSPORT PANNIER TANKS

LONDON TRANSPORT NUMBER	BR NUMBER	DATE BUILT	DATE SOLD TO LONDON TRANSPORT	WITHDRAWN BY LONDON TRANSPORT	FATE
L89	5775	1929	1963	1969	Sold To Keighley & Worth Valley Railway
L90 (I)	7711	1930	1956	1961	Scrapped
L90 (Ii)	7760	1930	1961	1971	Sold To 7029 Clun Castle Ltd
L91 (I)	5752	1929	1956	1960	Scrapped
L91 (Ii)	5757	1929	1960	1968	Scrapped
L92	5786	1930	1958	1969	Sold To Worcester Locomotive Society
L93	7779	1930	1958	1968	Scrapped
L94	7752	1930	1959	1971	Sold To 7029 Clun Castle Ltd
L95	5764	1929	1960	1971	Sold To The Severn Valley Railway
L96	7741	1930	1961	1967	Scrapped
L97	7749	1930	1962	1970	Scrapped
L98	7739	1929	1962	1970	Scrapped
L99	7715	1930	1963	1969	Sold To Quainton Railway Society

BELOW: Back in London Transport maroon livery, L99 hauls a short engineer's train past Kelling Heath during its loan spell at the North Norfolk Railway. BRIAN SHARPE

Chapter 6

London
Transport Museum

Covent Garden museum celebrates the transport that keeps the metropolis moving.

Underground railways and the steam locomotives that hauled early passenger trains are only one part of the multi-faceted story of how transport kept the mighty metropolis of London moving.

Since the days of the Romans, who founded a city at the narrowest and shallowest crossing point of the tidal Thames, London has been at the crux of western civilisation. It is a city where an empire was built, and where political decisions shaped the face of the globe.

Yet the key to the beating heart of the great metropolis is without a doubt its transport system; one of the most successful of any major city, anywhere.

How does a densely populated city of 8.63 million people (2015 figure) not grind to a halt?

You need a team of historians and transport planners to answer than one, for the movement of people on an hourly basis across London is a science unto itself.

This volume focuses on the role played by the Underground and the immeasurable contribution made, in particular, by the world's first subway line – the Metropolitan Railway.

London's transport system is a labyrinthine web, which has, over the centuries, involved boats and barges, horses and carts, horse buses, trams, hansom cabs, taxis, motor buses and surface railways, as well as those burrowing beneath the streets of the city centre.

To explore how London owes its prosperity to its transport network, and in doing so became a major world leader, there is only one port of call. London Transport Museum in Covent Garden.

One of the finest museums of its kind anywhere, this registered charity performs on a daily basis the colossal task of not only preserving artefacts from London's transport history, but also explaining how it all works.

The museum's main facility is located in a Victorian iron and glass building that had originally formed part of the Covent Garden vegetable, fruit and flower market.

Situated between Russell, Tavistock and Wellington streets and the east side of the former market square, it was designed as a dedicated flower market by William Rogers in 1871.

A hundred years later and the market had moved out and by 1980 the building was occupied by the London Transport Museum, moving from its base at Syon Park. The museum's collection had previously been housed in the British Transport Museum in a disused tram depot in Clapham High Street between 1963 and 1972. The railway locomotives and rolling stock from which were moved to the new National Railway Museum in York in the mid-Seventies.

Most of the Covent Garden museum's exhibits came from the collection of London Transport, but, since the creation of Transport for London in 2000, its remit expanded to cover all aspects of transportation in the city.

The first parts of the collection were brought together at the start of the 20th century by the London General Omnibus Company, which had the vision to preserve buses that were being retired from service.

When the company was taken over by the London Electric Railway, the heritage collection was enlarged to include rail vehicles. It continued to expand after the

ABOVE: The entrance to London Transport Museum in Covent Garden Piazza. LONDON TRANSPORT MUSEUM

ABOVE: The plush interior of coach No. 400: would it stand the wear and tear from today's public? ROBIN JONES

ABOVE: Metropolitan Railway bogie coach No. 400, built in 1900 when services were still hauled by steam. Behind it stands Metropolitan Railway Bo-Bo electric No. 5 *John Hampden*. ROBIN JONES

ABOVE: The museum's London Underground 1938 tube stock set is housed in Acton depot but used for special excursions over the system. ROBIN JONES

ABOVE: This low-sided wooded-bodied wagon, No. 306, was one of 100 ordered by the Metropolitan Railway in 1897. London Transport renumbered it in 1937 as ballast wagon 214. It was used in engineers' trains until the mid-Seventies, and was all but certain to have been hauled by red panniers. ROBIN JONES

ABOVE: A roundel-themed laser light show on the floor of the Covent Garden museum. ROBIN JONES

LER became part of the London Passenger Transport Board in the Thirties, and is still growing today.

Historic vehicles, world-famous posters and the finest objects from the museum's extraordinary collection are brought together to tell the story of London's development and the part transport played in defining its unique identity.

Just as the NRM in York has an outreach station in the Locomotion museum at Shildon in County Durham, so London Transport Museum has 'overspill' facilities for some of its large exhibits, such as buses and railway vehicles. The London Transport Museum Depot is located in Acton and is rail connected to the Underground. It is open to the public only on special days, whereas the Covent

Garden main site is open every day.

The Acton depot was opened in October 1999 and accommodates the majority of the museum's collections not on display in the main museum in Covent Garden.

It is the base for the museum's curators and conservators and provides 6000sq m of storage in secure, environmentally controlled conditions and houses more than 370,000 ▶

ABOVE: Poster art extraordinaire: Where is this bower beside the silver Thames? by Jean Dupas, 1930. LONDON TRANSPORT MUSEUM RIGHT: For the zoo book to Regent's Park, by Charles Paine, 1921. LONDON TRANSPORT MUSEUM

ABOVE: The museum's collection includes this scale model of North London Railway 2-4-0 No. 17. The North London opened in 1850 as a freight line linking the docklands to the main line railways, but soon added passenger trains, running from the City to Richmond. In 1855, the NLR bought 2-4-0 tank engines for its passenger service, which lasted until William Adams introduced 4-4-0Ts. ROBIN JONES

ABOVE: Roundels galore in store at Acton depot. ROBIN JONES

LEFT: West Ham Corporation Tramways 1910-built double-deck electric tram No. 102. ROBIN JONES

ABOVE: This unusual vehicle shedded in Acton depot was used for de-icing conductor rails. It was constructed at Acton Works in 1940 by combining two 1904-built Central London Railway motor cars. ROBIN JONES

items of all types, including many original works of art the biggest being a complete 1938 tube stock train.

The museum has one of the finest poster archives in the world. Since Frank Pick commissioned the first graphic poster for London Underground in 1908, the company and its successors have kept copies of everything.

By the 1980s, when the collection was transferred to the museum, it contained more than 5000 printed posters and nearly 1000 original artworks. The collection has grown steadily ever since, and is a treasure trove covering a century of British graphic design.

Pick's progressive commissioning policy led to more than 40 posters a year, and during the Twenties and Thirties, Underground railway posters reached a peak of aesthetic style. By 1933, London Transport was regarded as a leading patron of the arts.

For anyone seriously interested in transport, or simply wanting to indulge in nostalgia about the trains and buses of the past, it is a must-visit attraction. There is an excellent shop containing books and merchandise relating to every aspect of London's transport, and a superb cafe.

Throughout the year, the museum hosts a variety of special events. To find out more, visit its website at www.ltmuseum.co.uk ●

ABOVE: A 1932 poster highlighting the work on the Southgate extension of the Piccadilly Line. LONDON TRANSPORT MUSEUM

RIGHT: Now is the season of the year, 1925. The Covent Garden holds major exhibitions based around its massive poster collection. LONDON TRANSPORT MUSEUM

LONDON 2026 A.D. — THIS IS ALL IN THE AIR

TO·DAY — THE SOLID COMFORT OF THE UNDERGROUND

ABOVE: London 2026 AD; this is all in the air, by Montague B Black, 1926. LONDON TRANSPORT MUSEUM

UNDERGROUND

EASTCOTE
By DISTRICT RAILWAY

ABOVE: Eastcote by District Railway, by Charles Pears, published by Underground Electric Railways Company Ltd, 1913. LONDON TRANSPORT MUSEUM

ABOVE: London Transport K2 class trolleybus No. 1253, registration EXV253, was built in 1939. ROBIN JONES

ABOVE: A replica of the pioneering George Shillibeer's long-bodied horse bus, which ran from 1829, and was both his and London's first omnibus. The London General Omnibus Company ordered the replica to be built for the 1929 Omnibus Centenary Parade. ROBIN JONES

ABOVE: The K-type bus was a landmark design in which extra passenger space was created by adopting forward control with the driver alongside the engine. It could carry 46 passengers, 12 more than the B-type, despite being no longer or heavier. The first vehicles entered service in August 1919 and within two years, 1065 had been produced. No. K424, registration XC8059, was built in 1921 and worked routes in south London. It was withdrawn from Hounslow in 1932. ROBIN JONES

LEFT: London General Omnibus Company 1911-built B-type bus No. B340, registration LA 9928, inside the Covent Garden museum. ROBIN JONES

RIGHT: London Tramways Company double-deck horse tram No. 284, built by John Stephenson & Co of New York in 1882, inside the Covent Garden museum. ROBIN JONES

Chapter 7

Metropolitan Railway
E class No. 1

Carrying the torch for the Metropolitan Railway today is E class 0-4-4T No.1, the only steam locomotive that is still operational. Yet its survival is down to the actions of a 19-year-old apprentice at Neasden Works in 1962.

ABOVE: Met No. 1 in London Transport service as L44. LONDON TRANSPORT MUSEUM

The flagship of the historic Metropolitan Railway today is undoubtedly E class 0-4-4T No. 1.

However, despite its number, it was by far from being the first locomotive owned by the company.

The class was designed by the Chief Mechanical Engineer of the Met, TF Clark, for use on the Baker Street to Verney Junction service.

No. 1 was built in 1898 – a replacement for A class 4-4-0T No.1, which had been scrapped after an accident at Baker Street, at the junction of what is now the Inner Circle, and given its number.

A total of seven locomotives were built between 1896 and 1901 for the Met, three by the railway at its Neasden Works and four by the Hawthorn Leslie Company in Newcastle-upon-Tyne.

No. 1 was the last locomotive constructed at Neasden. The other E class members were numbered 77 to 82.

No. 77 was fitted with condensing apparatus for working inside the tube tunnels and it is likely that it was originally fitted to the whole class, but later removed.

On July 4, 1904, decorated with flags and bunting, No.1 headed the first passenger train on the opening of the Uxbridge branch from Harrow-on-the-Hill.

The electrification programme made more engines of the same type unnecessary and also led to the removal of the condensing apparatus. Class members were displaced from the main passenger trains by H class 4-4-4Ts in 1920, moving to lesser jobs such as services on the Chesham branch, freight workings and engineering duties. Following the Second World War, an E class locomotive was regularly stationed at Rickmansworth station to cover a failure of LNER engines working Metropolitan Line trains north of that point.

The first of the E class was scrapped in 1935 before it could be given a new London Transport number – No.1 became L44, while numbers 77, 80 and 81 became L46-L48.

The E class locomotives often worked permanent-way trains from Neasden, sometimes reaching Aylesbury to run round and take water. L44 was recorded at Aylesbury on a permanent-way train on August 21, 1955.

L44 worked the final steam train on the Chesham branch in July 1960 and the last steam-hauled London Transport passenger train anywhere in 1961, surviving in use until 1965.

The E4 was saved from scrapping by 19-year-old London Transport mechanical engineering apprentice, Jim Stringer, who established the Met Tank Appeal Fund in 1962.

He later recounted the events from the winter of 1961-62: "One of the warmest places to be was the steam shed. This was where I could generally be found – talking to the locomotive drivers, firemen and fitters when I was not working in the freezing cold, helping my fitter change a compressor or motor generator under a snow-encrusted Metropolitan Line T Stock train.

"It was here that I learned of London Transport's intention to scrap its fleet of superannuated steam locomotives and replace them with more ex-GWR 0-6-0 pannier tanks or battery locomotives.

"I believed that London Transport's action in scrapping these locomotives was rather short-sighted and that at least one of them should be kept for preservation.

"As London Transport was not intending to save one of these locomotives, I decided that I would try to save one myself. On the advice of Gerald Fitzgerald, one of the fitters, the locomotive chosen was L52, an F class 0-6-2T built in 1901 by the Yorkshire Engine Company, which was the last of its class to have survived. A price of £500 was agreed with London Transport to prevent it from going for scrap.

"It was at this point that I contacted the London Railway Preservation Society, which was keen to help and could also provide somewhere for the locomotive to go if we were successful.

"The Met Tank Appeal Fund was set up to raise the amount needed and during the months that followed, more than £1000 was collected from individuals keen to see it saved. One such contributor was C Hamilton Ellis, the well-known railway author and artist.

"However, when I came to hand over the cheque, I was advised that on inspection, L52 was found to have a cracked mainframe, so could no longer be steamed and was therefore not a viable option for preservation.

"It was suggested, however, that a better locomotive for me to purchase would be L44.

This locomotive was offered to me at the lower price of £450." It was withdrawn after taking part in the Metropolitan Centenary parade at Neasden on May 23, 1963, in which it hauled four bogie coaches and a milk van."

Even after purchasing L44, Jim had to wait for more than a year before permission could be granted to take it over BR metals in steam, as there was concern that the smoke could cause corrosion to the London Midland Region's overhead power lines. Jim recalled: "A campaign of support by my local newspaper, The Acton Gazette, may have helped smooth the way, and on Friday, March 20, 1964, L44 was finally moved under its own steam from Neasden to its new home.

"It had been agreed locally that I should travel some of the way on the footplate, but with several others crowding the limited space in the cab, I was only able to travel as far as Wembley Park."

The London Railway Preservation Society had arranged storage for the locomotive at Skimpot Lane, Luton. The society had been founded in 1962 to ▶

ABOVE: The locomotive that was not saved: a London Transport publicity picture of F class 0-6-2T L2 at Neasden in 1961. In the picture are would-be saviour Jim Stringer, who instead saved L44 (No. 1) and Neasden fitter Gerald Fitzgerald, who helped him. LT

BELOW: As L44, Met No. 1 heads a rake of four Ashbury coaches and a milk van at the Neasden centenary parade in 1963. LONDON TRANSPORT MUSEUM

ABOVE: L44 at Neasden shortly before moving off into preservation. JIM STRINGER COLLECTION

preserve artefacts representing the capital's railway heritage. It bought a series of former London Underground vehicles and collectables and built up a large collection of LNWR memorabilia.

The items were at first temporarily stored at depots in Luton and Bishop's Stortford, but as space became short, the society began to look for a permanent home and considered several sites before choosing Quainton Road station on the former Great Central Railway main line, which had closed to through trains on September 3, 1966, as part of the Beeching cuts.

Quainton Road itself had closed to passengers on March 4, 1963 and to goods on July 4, 1966. The GCR route from Aylesbury to Rugby was abandoned on September 3 that year, leaving just the GCR line from Aylesbury to Calvert on the Oxford-Bletchley line, and using a spur line installed in 1942 at Calvert Junction, open for freight. The line was singled shortly afterwards, and the signalbox at Quainton Road was abandoned on August 13, 1967, when the points connecting to the goods yard were disconnected.

The Quainton Railway Society Ltd was formed in 1969 and the London Railway Preservation Society was formally incorporated into it on April 24, 1971. The society was granted charitable status the following year, and became known as the Buckinghamshire Railway Centre.

Met No. 1 was moved to Aylesbury in 1968, and was stored there for two years. It was transferred by rail to Quainton Road on September 23, 1970, with a track slew from the British Rail main line into the Down yard.

As the station did not have any covered accommodation when the society first moved to the site, a building was erected in the Down yard, spanning 150ft long tracks, and incorporating workshops, a museum and refreshments facility.

The station became a bookshop and ticket office, while the extensive sidings, which had been disconnected from the main line in 1967, were used for locomotive restoration. The society eventually restored the main station building to its turn-of-the-19th-century appearance.

Another building was acquired from London Transport and relocated to Quainton from Wembley Park station. It became known as the Wembley Shed and houses engines and carriages awaiting restoration. A 60ft turntable was also later installed.

There are no regular passenger train services at the centre, but rides are offered along two running lines in the yards either side of the working Network Rail line, which runs through the middle of the centre, and is regularly used by landfill trains running from waste transfer depots in Greater London to the former brick pits at Calvert.

The main station building is on the Up side of the Network Rail line with a smaller wooden building on the platform between the currently vacant Down line trackbed and the platform from which the Brill branch ran, as described in Chapter 4.

The first major overhaul of No. 1 began on August 13, 1975 with the removal of the tanks and cab, followed by the boiler being lifted in February 1976.

Following its overhaul at Quainton, No. 1 was maintained to the standard required for British Rail main line running. ●

ABOVE: Larking around, but don't worry, L44 was stationary with the brake on! Jim Stringer lies in a shed siding at Neasden shed while fellow apprentices Tom Ward (left) and Peter Pearson trying to 'run him over' by hand. JIM STRINGER COLLECTION

Metropolitan Tank Locomotive Appeal

Engine No. L.52 'F' Class 0-6-2.

An appeal has been launched by a large body of railway enthusiasts to preserve L.52 the last remaining 'F' Class Tank Locomotive belonging to the London Transport Board based at Neasden Depot.

This Engine was first put on line in 1901 for hauling mixed traffic on the Metropolitan Railway, and was last employed in 1961.

The sum of £500 is required to purchase it for preservation for the benefit of our future generation.

We are now appealing to you railway enthusiasts or as a member of the travelling public, to contribute a small donation towards obtaining the necessary funds to conclude the purchase deal with the London Transport Executive.

This appeal is issued in conjunction with the London Railway Preservation Society who have agreed to take custody of the Engine. It will be placed on the Vintage Railway which this Society plan to operate in the countryside convenient to North London.

All Contributions should be by means of crossed postal order or cheque and made out to "THE MET TANK APPEAL".

ALL MONEY OR CORRESPONDENCE
SHOULD BE ADDRESSED TO ▶

J. C. STRINGER, ESQ.
2 GIBBON ROAD,
ACTON, LONDON, W.3.

ABOVE: Met No. 1 heads the first train into Uxbridge, the terminus of the new branch, on July 4, 1904. LONDON TRANSPORT MUSEUM

RIGHT: The Met Tank Appeal Fund leaflet. At this stage, it was not known that L52 had a cracked main frame, and that L44 (No. 1) would be chosen instead. JIM STRINGER COLLECTION

BELOW: Met No. 1 in steam at Quainton Road station on October 8, 2006. ROBIN JONES

Chapter 8

Steam on the Met:
First time round

A plan to celebrate the centenary of Metro-land's Chesham branch in 1989 quickly mushroomed into a hugely popular annual event with a far wider Underground remit, which saw steam locomotives from the Big Four main line companies haul services over the Metropolitan Line in-between standard electric tube services.

As on the national railway network, which is considered a separate entity from London Underground, enthusiast groups' steam-hauled specials became commonplace in the Fifties.

On July 4, 1954, to mark the 50th anniversary of the Uxbridge line, an anniversary train headed by none other than L44 – which as Met No. 1 had hauled the inaugural train half a century before – ran from Baker Street to Uxbridge returning via South Harrow and High Street Kensington.

L44 was in action again on May 22, 1955, heading part of a Railway World special from Baker Street to Stanmore and Chesham, coming on at Rickmansworth.

On June 3, 1956, the 'John Milton Special', a ramblers' excursion, was hauled by sister L48 from Rickmansworth to Chesham and back.

Another E class locomotive, L46, headed a Stephenson Locomotive Society Circle and Hammersmith & City tour on September 22, 1957, from Hammersmith via Edgware Road, South Kensington and Liverpool Street to Wembley Park.

On October 1, 1961, a Southern Counties Touring Society special was worked by L44 from Wembley Park to Stanmore, Baker Street and New Cross Gate. It was the last steam-worked passenger train over any part of the Circle Line.

British Railways' steam locomotives also ventured off the national network on to Underground metals to head tours. The Locomotive Club of Great Britain's Poplar & Edgware tour on May 5, 1956, was steam worked over the Northern Line from East Finchley to Mill Hill East en route to Edgware (Great Northern) and back.

On September 28, 1958, an 'Essex Wealdman' ramblers' trip was steam worked from Liverpool Street to Ongar and back.

September 9, 1961, saw a London Transport farewell to steam trip run from Baker Street to Amersham and back, being steam worked return from Rickmansworth to Amersham.

BELOW: WR 0-6-0PT No. 9466 crosses the Grand Union Canal at Watford on July 1, 1989. This colourful spot was a favourite among Steam on the Met lineside cameramen. BRIAN SHARPE

The LCGB's Great Eastern Suburban Tour ran on both April 7 and 28, 1962, to Ongar and back, and on May 26, 1963, a London Transport centenary special ran from Baker Street to Aylesbury, returning via Watford. It was steam worked from Amersham to Aylesbury and back. This section of the Met was by then owned by British Railways, but the train was run by London Transport with its own stock.

ABOVE: Restored to its 1903 condition, Metropolitan Railway A class 0-4-0T is seen with a pair of wagons in the line's centenary parade at Neasden in May 1963. The S&K wagons recall Smith & Knight, the contractors who built much of the line. LONDON TRANSPORT MUSEUM

ABOVE: No. 1 on show at the Neasden parade on May 23, 1963. WHR GODWIN/LONDON TRANSPORT MUSEUM

ABOVE RIGHT: Met No. 1 hauls milk van no. 3, restored to its Metropolitan Railway style and four ex-Metropolitan coaches at the Neasden centenary open day parade on May 23, 1963. The coaches, which worked in their latter years on the Chesham branch, were sold to the Bluebell Railway, but more of them and this train in Chapter 13. WHR GODWIN/LONDON TRANSPORT MUSEUM

ABOVE: LNER B12 4-6-0 No. 61572 passes Pinner on May 25, 2000, running parallel with K1 2-6-0 No. 62005. JOHN STRETTON

THE CHESHAM CENTENARY

Around 1988, London Underground came up with the idea of holding a one-off event including steam trips to mark the centenary of the line from Rickmansworth to Chesham in July the following year.

The original idea was to run steam specials purely on the short Chesham branch from Amersham. However, it was soon agreed at various levels within London Underground that it was possible to operate steam trains between Chesham and Watford.

A team group was created from operations and engineering departments and other areas to arrange the ground-breaking service.

Apart from the one-off special tours, there had been no history of operating heritage steam on London Underground. The only model in existence was the national rail network, using main line steam crews to drive and fire the locomotives. Unfortunately London Underground had no history in this area, so a new way had to be found if steam trains were to operate on its metals.

The hiring of steam crews from the main line was beyond consideration as the costs were astronomic, requiring enormous amounts of training.

The organising group of Malcolm Dean, train services manager on the Metropolitan Line, Roger Paddison, fleet manager at Neasden, as well as Andy Barr, also from the operations department, agreed with HM Railway Inspectorate and the railway trade unions that private steam owners could drive their locomotives provided that they were accompanied on the footplate by drivers and a suitably qualified Operations Inspector.

The vehicles also had to meet London Underground engineering standards, and suitable operations training took place.

BELOW: The programme for the 1989 Chesham centenary steam specials, which began Steam on the Met. PHIL MARSH COLLECTION

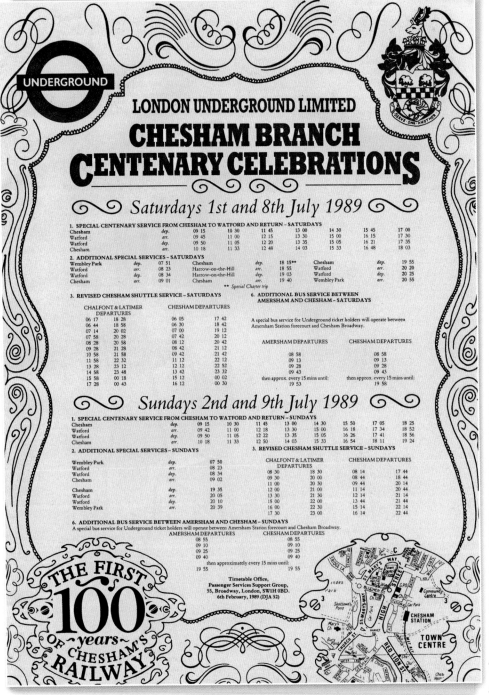

MET NO. 1 MAKES ITS COMEBACK

Of course, the first choice to haul the new generation of steam specials would be Metropolitan Railway E class 0-4-4T No. 1.

At its Buckinghamshire Railway Centre home. Met No.1 was maintained to the standard required for British Rail main line running, and also visited other lines, such as the Keighley & Worth Valley Railway in April 1994 – where it operated with that line's Metropolitan Railway Dreadnought coaches and the Mid Hants Railway in September 1987 for the Watercress Line's 10th anniversary.

The centre was asked if it could provide locomotives and steam crews for the event.

As run-round facilities on the route were no longer available, the trains would be steam hauled towards Chesham and hauled on the return to Watford by veteran Metropolitan Railway Bo-Bo electric locomotive No. 12 *Sarah Siddons*.

This locomotive was built by Metropolitan Vickers in 1921 as one of 20, and once worked express services including Pullman trains from Rickmansworth to Baker Street.

Indeed, it hauled passenger trains until 1961, when it was replaced by standard tube stock, but was one of four examples saved for Departmental use and refurbished in 1971 for special trains marking the end of London Underground steam.

There were to be nine return trips plus outward and homebound runs from and to Neasden depot where the train would be stored overnight. The event was to be staged over the weekends of July 1-2 and 6-9, 1989. Former London Transport 57XX pannier L99, now back in its GWR livery as No. 7715 and a shedmate of No.1 at Quainton Road, would be the standby locomotive.

The two steam locomotives were examined to British Rail specification by the Derby inspectorate. Met No. 1 was already logged on to its system, but L99 would have to be stripped, which would include removal of the boiler and detubing for a thorough internal examination.

Both locomotives had to be fitted with air braking equipment to make them compatible both with *Sarah Siddons* and the BR 4VEP electric multiple unit set that was to be used for the train.

As L99 was needed for Santa special steamings at the centre, its dismantling for inspection could not take place until the festive period was over. In the new year, the engine was completely dismantled within a few weeks but as work progressed it soon became clear that it was not in as a good condition as had been expected.

The boiler was completely stripped of tanks and fittings and was ready for inspection by the end of March – but the BR boiler inspector couldn't come to examine the boiler until the beginning of May. Met No. 1 needed several cracked wheel spokes repaired, again under BR supervision.

Both locomotives passed ultrasonic axle examinations.

However, when the boiler inspector finally arrived, he ordered all of L99's steel firebox

ABOVE: WR 94XX 0-6-0PT No. 9466 and Metropolitan E Class 0-4-4T No. 1 under the bridge at Harrow-on-the-Hill on July 27 during the 1990 Steam on the Met event. HEC TATE*

No. 9466 was built in 1952 by Robert Stephenson & Hawthorns in Newcastle-upon-Tyne, and was withdrawn on June 6, 1964 and sent, along with hundreds of other British Railways' steam locomotives, to Woodham Brothers' scrapyard in Barry, arriving there that November.

Unlike the 57XX panniers, neither it nor any other 94XX ever worked in London Transport services in pre-preservation days.

Its 11 years in the scrapyard were almost as long as its period in Western Region service. Bought for preservation, it moved to the Buckinghamshire Railway Centre on September 25, 1975, as the 74th locomotive to be moved out of Barry for use in the heritage sector. Dennis Howells acquired it in 1977.

It took eight years to return No. 9466 to steam. Over the past three decades, it has visited numerous heritage railways, and it is also maintained for main line operation, fitted in 2006 with Train Protection & Warning System and On-Train Monitoring and Recording apparatus. Indeed, it was the first 0-6-0 to have both systems fitted.

The GWR livery that it carried in the first Steam on the Met series was historically inappropriate, as No. 9466 had not been built in the GWR era.

No. 9466 underwent its first two seven-year main line overhauls at London Transport's Ruislip depot in 1993-94 and Neasden depot in May 2004.

stays to be replaced together with about 100 rivets. The job could not be done in time, and so L99 withdrew from the event.

However, a ready, willing and able replacement was found in Dennis Howell's Western Region 0-6-0 pannier No. 9466, which was also based at Quainton Road and had been working at Didcot Railway Centre. He agreed that it could become the spare

engine provided it was allowed to work the odd train in its own right.

A NEW BREED OF PANNIER FOR THE MET!
GWR Chief Mechanical Engineer Frederick Hawksworth's taper-boiler evolution of the 57XX – the 94XX class – had got to 210 members built between 1947 and 1956, production ceasing with dieselisation.

THE UNEXPECTED STAR

Training for the Quainton Road crews took place at Neasden depot on June 11 and 18, 1989, many of them not being used to air-braked trains.

Each session finished with a road learning trip along the route of the specials to familiarise drivers and firemen with the location of signals, stations and gradients.

Met No. 1 arrived at the former Neasden steam shed by road on June 19, and steamed the following day for another BR examination, with Thames TV cameras present.

No. 9466 arrived by rail from Didcot in time for the first test run, comprising Didcot's BR Mk.1 chocolate-and-cream support coach and several London Underground wagons headed by a battery locomotive.

Met No. 1 and No. 9466 were coupled to the rear and in the early hours after service trains had finished, the test train departed Neasden for Chesham via Watford.

However, a quick inspection at Watford showed that No.1 had run a hot axlebox. It was taken off the test train and moved into a siding while the 94XX pannier took the train to Chesham. No. 1 was slowly worked back to Neasden under its own steam, after Underground staff fixed up a water supply at Watford until a pilotman and inspector could arrive.

The axlebox was removed, and the Ffestiniog Railway remetalled and machined the box at its Boston Lodge Works.

Far from doing the odd trip, No. 9466 went on to handle the entire first weekend's programme of trains.

The following week, the repaired axlebox was returned from Wales and No.1 was lowered back on to its wheels and returned to steam.

A test run to Ruislip depot was arranged, but on arrival, several battery locomotives had been parked in front of the depot entrance. No. 1 had to continue to Uxbridge sidings, which are

ABOVE: WR 94XX 0-6-0PT No. 9466, Met No. 1 and London Transport battery locomotive L94, at Harrow-on-the-Hill on July 28, 1990. HEC TATE*

ABOVE: BR 4MT Standard 2-6-4T No. 80080 from the Midland Railway-Butterley drifts down the gradient at Chalfont and Latimer on July 28, 1990. HEC TATE*

ABOVE: A Steam on the Met triple-header on July 28, 1990: WR 0-6-0PT No. 9466, Met No. 1 and London Transport battery locomotive L44 approach Harrow-on-the-Hill. L44 was the number carried by No.1 in its London Transport era. HEC TATE*

ABOVE: BR Standard 4MT 2-6-4T No. 80080 at Chorleywood station on July 27, 1990. HEC TATE*

located the site of the original Uxbridge station opened by Met No. 1 in 1904.

Returning to Neasden for water, a second trip to Ruislip was made, again with the Didcot support coach. The following day, No. 1 hauled a loaded 150-ton train to Ruislip, commuters looking bemused as it climbed the 1-in-30 gradient into Wembley Park station.

Finally, on Saturday, July 8, 1989, exactly 100 years after the branch opened, Met No. 1 made it back into Chesham station. That weekend, all of the scheduled trains ran.

AN ANNUAL EVENT

There was a pause in the service in 1991, as it was a busy year professionally for the organisers, and there was no time available. However, this allowed effective planning to be put in place for 1992.

As Met No. 1 was not then free, two locomotives and their crews from heritage railways were invited to attend. These were LMS 'Black Five' 4-6-0 No. 44932 and LNER N7 0-6-2T No. 69621.

Two former London Transport panniers – L90 (7760) and L99 – returned in 1993 for Steam on the Met, as the event had by then become known. Also running was LMS 2-6-0 No. 46441.

Services that year operated from Amersham and to Harrow. Also as part of the event, there was a celebration of District 150 using L99 to return to its old haunts at Ealing Common.

The 90th anniversary of the opening of the Harrow to Uxbridge line in 1994 was marked by steam trips to both Amersham and Uxbridge using L99 again, and BR Standard 4MT 2-6-4T No. 80079, with LNER N2 0-6-2T No. 69523. The service again operated from Amersham to Harrow.

Crowds flocked to the events each year, which were logistically complicated for London Underground as it had to run the steam services in-between the normal Metropolitan and Chiltern services. A special set of coaches was acquired for the event.

In 1995, an innovation was introduced with parallel running on the local line and the fast lines between Harrow and Moor Park on the early and late trains to and from Neasden, as well as an Amersham to Harrow service.

Indeed, parallel running became the best-remembered feature of the first Steam on the Met series.

The locomotives involved in 1995 were No. 80079. No. 9466 and BR Standard 4MT No. 75014. *Sarah Siddons* suffered a hot axlebox and was replaced with a battery locomotive.

In 1996, the steam service was revised to Watford to Amersham, with the first and last trains starting and finishing at Harrow. Parallel running was again an attraction of the event for linesiders. The locomotives were No. 75014, No. 9466 and GWR 2-6-0 No. 7325.

In 1997 there was no steam service, but in 1998 it returned to enjoy glorious weather. Locomotives used were LMS 2-6-0 No. 2968 and LNER B1 4-6-0 No. 1264 *Mayflower*, the latter replaced by the 94XX when a defect was found after the first weekend.

For many, 1999 was one of the best Steam on the Met events, with No. 9466 starring alongside Southern Railway U class 2-6-0 No. 31625, LMS 'Black Five' No. 45110 and LNER K1 2-6-0 No. 62005. Met No. 1, now needing an overhaul, was displayed at Rickmansworth, keeping the flag flying for its parent company on its home ground.

BELOW: Parallel running with BR Standard 4MT 4-6-0 No. 75014 and 4MT 2-6-4T No. 80079 between Harrow and Moor Park on May 28, 1995. BRIAN SHARPE

ABOVE: LMS 'Black Five' 4-6-0 No. 44932 departs from Harrow on May 17, 1992. BRIAN SHARPE

ABOVE: LNER K1 2-6-0 No. 62005 at sunset on May 20, 1999, before the Steam on the Met test run for that year's event. PHIL MARSH

ABOVE: GER N7 0-6-2T No. 69621 departs from Harrow-on-the-Hill for Amersham on May 17, 1992 during London Transport's Steam on the Met event. BRIAN SHARPE

ABOVE: Out in the open: pannier L99 on a night test run from Neasden to Ealing on June 5, 1993. PHIL MARSH

LEFT: Two former London Transport panniers – L90 (7760) and L99 (7715) – returned to the electrified lines in 1993 for Steam on the Met. ANDY BARR

BELOW: Inside No. 12 Sarah Siddons during a test run on May 18, 1994. PHIL MARSH

ABOVE: Vintage Metropolitan Railway Bo-Bo electric No. 12 Sarah Siddons under the moonlight as it completes a test run from Neasden to Ealing depots on June 5, 1993. PHIL MARSH

▶

ABOVE: GWR 57XX 0-6-0PT L99 on a night train transfer movement at Baker Street station on May 10, 1994.

ABOVE: Pannier L99 in a very smoky Baker Street station during a Neasden to Ealing test run on June 5, 1993. PHIL MARSH

ABOVE: Great Eastern Railway N2 0-6-2T No. 69523 on a sunset test run on May 18, 1994. PHIL MARSH

ABOVE: GWR prairie No. 4144 heads into Chorleywood on May 16, 1998. COLOUR-RAIL

BELOW: Severn Valley Railway-based BR standard 4MT 2-6-4T No. 80079 at Uxbridge on May 28, 1995. COLOUR-RAIL

ABOVE: The Buckinghamshire Railway Centre's pannier L99 (7715) at Ealing depot after a night Steam on the Met test run on June 5, 1993. PHIL MARSH

LEFT: LNER K1 2-6-0 No. 62005 crosses the Grand Union Canal, departing from Watford during Steam on the Met on May 22. 1999. JOHN TITLOW

ABOVE: The crew of Dennis Howell's Western Region pannier No. 9466 at Amersham on May 12, 1996. PHIL MARSH

ABOVE: Ivatt 2-6-2T No. 41312 from the Mid Hants Railway and pannier No. 9466 at Croxley on May 21, 2000. COLOUR-RAIL

THE LAST YEAR

The last year of Steam on the Met was 2000, and it saw No. 9466, LNER B12 4-6-0 No. 61572, LMS Ivatt 2-6-2T No. 41312 and No. 62005 in action.

It bought to an end a superb and memorable series of operations that gave great pleasure to the travelling public, Underground staff and engine owners alike, raising thousands of pounds for charity in the process.

The division of London Underground Limited into separate infrastructure and operating companies as well as a feeling that the event was diverting resources from the Underground's core business were to blame for the decision to stop running the event.

Steam on the Met was unique, a triumph in the preservation world and a halfway house between heritage railways and main line railtours.

On the one hand the shuttle services were operated by volunteer crews, but ran side by side with an intensive main line service demanding high speeds and tight timings. And it all worked out, because of the drive and perseverance of individuals; the willingness of many staff to give up their time to assist, and the helpfulness of engine owners all contributed to its success.

The greatest thanks of all go to the London Underground senior management team, which took an informed risk of normal train services being delayed. However, in the 12 years of Steam on the Met, no major disruption to regular passenger services took place.

Sheer professionalism on all sides.

ABOVE: Southern Railway U class 2-6-0 No. 31625 from the Mid Hants Railway during a test run on the Met on May 20, 1999. PHIL MARSH

ABOVE: Parallel running in 1995 between Severn Valley Railway-based BR standard 4MT 2-6-4T No. 80079, and BR standard 4-6-0 No. 75014, which is now owned by the Dartmouth Steam Railway. From the mid-Nineties onwards, parallel running was the highlight of Steam on the Met for many enthusiasts. ANDY BARR

ABOVE: Static display only this time round: out-of-ticket Met No. 1 is towed from Neasden to Rickmansworth on May 20, 1999. PHIL MARSH

Chapter 9

Fresh stirrings
in the forest

Plant an acorn, and mighty oaks will one day appear. The beginning of the return of steam-hauled passenger trains to London Underground took root in a forgotten colliery building at Bream in the heart of the Forest of Dean, 136 miles from Baker Street....

RIGHT: Charted surveyor, Bill Parker, who founded the Flour Mill workshop, is a market leader in the restoration of Victorian steam locomotives. ROBIN JONES

BELOW: The National Collection's sole-surviving LSWR T9 'Greyhound' No. 30120 was restored to running order by the Flour Mill workshop. Built in 1899 and therefore a year younger than Met No. 1, the T9, a veteran of the North Cornwall line to Padstow, is seen at Boscarne at its current Bodmin & Wenford Railway home on September 9, 2010, the day it was officially launched back into traffic. It was the success of restorations such as this that led to London Transport Museum choosing the Flour Mill for the overhaul of No. 1 for the Met 150 celebrations. ROBIN JONES

In 1986, British Rail Engineering Limited decided to close Isambard Kingdom Brunel's GWR workshops at Swindon. The announcement devastated the great railway town, but the legacy of steam was not finished yet.

Chartered surveyor Bill Parker, an enthusiast since his boyhood days who had made his fortune in the USA, met up with old friend Ivor Huddy, a works employee who had previously helped him buy two steam locomotives. The pair hatched a plan to save at least part of the works where steam locomotives could continue to be maintained.

British Rail eventually sold the works site to Tarmac Properties, and Bill agreed a deal to get the lathes rolling again.

The new Swindon Railway Workshop was owned by Swindon Heritage Trust, a charitable trust, which was was allowed to occupy up to four acres of buildings.

In 1989 it was becoming apparent that the National Railway Museum would have to find a home for much of its collection while the roof of its main building at York was replaced.

With some difficulty, Bill persuaded Tarmac to allow the works to be used as a temporary home for much of the National Collection.

The 1990 'National Railway Museum of tour' exhibition at Swindon saw masterpieces

ABOVE: The National Railway Museum's working replica of Stephenson's *Rocket* took part in the Great Central Railway's spring bank holiday weekend 2010 Golden Oldies gala, featuring replica locomotives from the early years of steam. Following its thorough rebuild at the Flour Mill workshops, wheels and cylinders apart, the *Rocket* replica is a new locomotive. ROBIN JONES

such as GWR 4-6-0 No. 6000 *King George V* and unofficial record breaker No. 3440 *City of Truro* displayed alongside BR Standard 9F 2-1-0 No. 92220 *Evening Star* and the fastest steam locomotive in the world, Gresley A4 Pacific No. 4468 *Mallard*.

Bill had been introduced to the late Princess of Wales, who told him that her children William and Harry were "mad on trains", and inevitably an invitation to Swindon followed. The princes stayed for two hours: climbing up on the bufferbeam of *King George V*, and riding precariously on the back of the works traction engine up to *City of Truro*.

It had been hoped that the heritage version of Swindon works would become permanent. However, when the 'Thatcher boom' of the late 1980s bust and the value of commercial developments collapsed, Tarmac gave Swindon Railway Workshop notice to quit.

Protests and bad publicity eventually forced a U-turn by the landowner, but by then the relationship between Bill Parker and the Tarmac Properties management had broken down completely; Tarmac subsequently agreed a deal with the trust's former works manager, Bill Jefferies, and Hull businessman Ken Ryder, to take up a tenancy inside the works.

The pair established a new operation entitled Swindon Locomotive Carriage & Wagon Works, which in turn was taken over by engineer Steve Atkins, who rebranded it as Swindon Railway Engineering.

Meanwhile, the original Swindon Heritage Trust remained without a home until 1994 when Bill bought a semi-derelict engine house at Flour Mill Colliery at Bream in the Forest of Dean, a Grade II listed building dating from 1908.

It was restored with the help of a grant from the Rural Development Commission and the trust began operations again – initially, still trading under the name of Swindon Railway Workshop, even though it lay in deepest Gloucestershire, the county nextdoor to Wiltshire.

SWINDON WORKS REBORN!

The Flour Mill opened as a railway workshop on July 1, 1996. The 'new' Swindon Works' first job, ironically, was overhauling the National Railway Museum's replica Gooch broad gauge 4-2-2 *Iron Duke*, which was completed in time for museum's annual dinner in September 1996.

The workshop team then completed the rebuilding of GWR 0-6-0 pannier tank No. 4612 from little more than a pile of spare parts, frames, a boiler and wheels, two of them with spokes cut, after the engine was bought from Barry scrapyard after having been used as a 'donor' locomotive to keep sister No. 5775 running on the Keighley & Worth Valley Railway. Its eventual sale to the Bodmin & Wenford Railway Trust, negotiated by Bill with retired London banker and that railway's prime sponsor Alan Moore, who funded it, led to a partnership that continues to this day.

The trust then won the contract to carry out the NRM's replica Stephenson's *Rocket's* 10-year boiler overhaul, which was also completed to a tight schedule.

Various private owners soon became aware that something was stirring in the forest, and began enquiring about bringing locomotives in for maintenance, repair, or long-term overhaul as and when funds permitted.

The building, about 100ft long, has no rail connection to the main line, with the existing rails laid on an old 1825 tramway trackbed, and can be reached only by a road though the woods.

Although the Flour Mill is capable of overhauling engines of any size (the two largest so far being David Shepherd's 9F No. 92203 *Black Prince* and most of WR 4-60 No. 6960 *Raveningham Hall*) it is ideally suited to medium-sized engines, and to some extent has specialised in tank engines – as Bill says "more Caerphilly or Wolverhampton than Swindon"!

The relationship with the National Railway Museum developed with the urgent repair ▶

ABOVE: This Grade II listed colliery building is home to the Flour Mill workshop. ROBIN JONES

of Captain Bill Smith's GNR J52 0-6-0 No. 68846 just in time for its centenary in 1999.

Then one of the two surviving London & South Western Railway Beattie well tanks, No. 30587, which is part of the National Collection but which had been on loan to the South Devon Railway, was returned to steam at the Flour Mill for use on the Bodmin & Wenford Railway, funded by Alan, after spending years on static display inside Buckfastleigh station museum.

The successful repair of this ancient and well-loved icon under the eagle eye of then NRM head of engineering, Richard Gibbon, and its triumphant return to steam at Bodmin in 2002 led to other similar work.

Not only did Alan fund the repair of the other surviving Beattie well tank, the Buckinghamshire Railway Centre's No. 30585, but in due course that of the NRM's LSWR T9 'Greyhound' 4-4-0 No. 30120, another Victorian (1899) engine that had problems previously considered too difficult to repair, in this case with its cylinder block. It too went to Bodmin after being resteamed at the Flour Mill.

When a deal for Tyseley Locomotive Works to repair the boiler of *City of Truro*

at a discounted price in time for the 2004 centenary of its unofficial 100mph record run, fell through, the Flour Mill and Alan Moore stepped in once more.

The partnership with Alan extended not only to repairs to the big GWR 2-8-0 tank, No. 4247, now also based at Bodmin, but to construction in 2009 of a new working replica of Stephenson's 1829 *Rocket* commissioned by the Science Museum, using only the driving wheels and cylinders recovered from the old one, with Alan funding the new boiler and Bill Parker the new frames.

By then, the Flour Mill had earned a reputation as market leader in the overhaul, repair and maintenance of Victorian locomotives.

STEAM ON THE MET: A REVIVAL?

It was in 2010 that talks began in the capital about how best to celebrate the 150th anniversary of London Underground, the world's oldest subway system.

Suggestions came from a variety of high-ranking figures – Sam Mullins, director of London Transport Museum, London Underground's chief operating officer Howard Collins, and the then Commissioner of Transport for London Sir Peter Hendy.

Various ideas were discussed, but they all began to move in one direction – a return of Steam of the Met, but in a more dynamic form.

This time round, it would not be confined to the surface lines of the Metropolitan Railway, but would run through the tunnels beneath the heart of London.

Most daring of all, a Victorian train of wooden-bodied coaches would be run behind a steam locomotive – carrying passengers in the middle of the day, the specials interspersed between modern electric tube trains.

There was a clear choice for the locomotive to haul the new generation of Underground steam specials – Metropolitan Railway E class 0-4-4T No. 1.

It was indeed an ambitious aim, and there would be much work to be done before final clearance could be given to run the steam

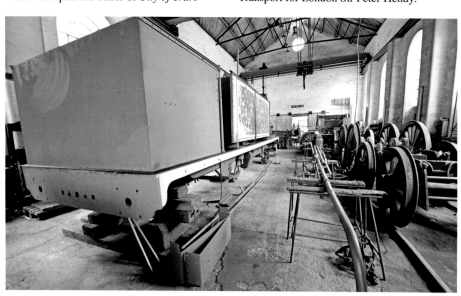

ABOVE: Met No. 1 inside the Flour Mill workshop and ready to be re-wheeled. ANDY BARR

specials on the tube network, not least of all being the practicality, let alone the demanding safety requirements.

One of the first steps was to approach the Buckinghamshire Railway Centre about the availability of No. 1, the boiler ticket of which had expired in August 2009. Centre officials agreed to allow investigative work of No. 1 to take place.

Chosen for that job was the Flour Mill, which had undertaken the previous overhaul of No. 1 in 2001 and so knew the engine well. The London Transport Museum, which also agreed to finance the transport costs, said that it would look at the results of the explorative study on No. 1 before deciding whether to release funding for its full restoration.

The study showed that No. 1 was again capable of restoration to a condition whereby it could haul trains at 50mph on the Underground, for a reasonable sum… and the Flour Mill workshop won the contract to overhaul it.

The museum subsequently launched a £250,000 appeal to cover the cost of the overhaul and the engine's operation on the Underground.

As events would turn out, not only would the Flour Mill repair No.1, but its steam drivers would provide the footplate crew to take it through the tunnels during the Metropolitan Railway celebrations, which had by then been scheduled for early 2013.

WORK IN PROGRESS

As part of the build up to Met 150, as the big event become popularly known, a private VIP party visited the Flour Mill on Saturday, August 18, 2012, to view progress on the restoration of Met No. 1.

The party included Peter Hendy, former Chiltern Railways' chairman, Adrian Shooter,

ABOVE: The VIP party, which visited the Flour Mill on August 18, 2012, to assess the preparations for the Metropolitan Railway 150 celebrations, stand in front of 'Willy' the well tank. ANDY BARR

and mega-enthusiast Sir William McAlpine and his wife Judy.

They saw stripped-down No. 1 waiting to be rewheeled, and heard Bill Parker tell the story of its restoration and Sam Mullins outline plans for the celebrations the following year.

The party also had an exclusive first viewing of the latest standard gauge steam locomotive to be restored in the heritage era.

Kerr Stuart 0-4-0WT No. 3063 was built in 1918 to a much older class of shunter design dating back to the 1860s.

Nicknamed 'Willy', it is similar to *The King*, and *Windle*, both of which are now on the Ribble Steam Railway.

The Admiralty bought 'Willy' for a First World War National Shipyard in Chepstow,

although the war ended before it could see active service.

The locomotive never left Chepstow and ended up working at the bridge-builders Fairfield-Mabey, along with the Great Eastern 'coffee-pot' 0-4-0ST No. 229, which was previously displayed at the now-closed North Woolwich Old Station Museum. For many years through the Sixties and Seventies they sat out of use clearly visible from the railway line at Chepstow, until purchased by Bill and his brother Richard in 1980.

'Willy' is now the works shunter at the Flour Mill. Meanwhile the work carries on – the last job finished was the Telford Steam Railway's GWR 0-6-2T No. 5619, now also at Bodmin, while work continues on Rob May's Polish Ferrum Tkh 0-6-0T *Karel* and No. 229. ●

BELOW: The Telford Steam Railway's GWR 0-6-2T No. 5619, which last steamed in spring 2014, is hauled out of the Flour Mill workshops at Bream in the Forest of Dean following repairs, by works shunter Kerr Stuart 0-4-0WT No. 3063 of 1918 'Willy', before going on loan to the Bodmin & Wenford Railway for the summer. BILL PARKER

Chapter 10

In the still of
the night

In secret, a steam train ran beneath the streets of London early on the morning of Sunday, February 26, 2012. The National Railway Museum's London & South Western Railway Beattie well tank No. 30587 returned steam to the tunnels of London Underground as a test run to pave the way for major celebrations to mark the 150th anniversary of the Metropolitan Railway, the world's first underground line, in 2013.

On the afternoon of Thursday, February 23, 2012, an Allelys low-loader completed its journey from the heart of Cornwall to west London.

On its trailer was one of two surviving LSWR Beattie 2-4-0 well tanks, locomotives built for London suburban lines around the same time that the Metropolitan Railway was in its infancy.

No. 30587, one of three members of the class that saw out their days on the Wenfordbridge mineral branch on the western side of Bodmin Moor, hauling china clay trains, had been a member of the Bodmin & Wenford Railway's regular fleet since the Flour Mill restored it to running order in 2002.

Now it had come home to London, on a mission impossible.

Under a shroud of utmost secrecy, the Flour Mill loco crew – who were otherwise busy overhauling Met No. 1 – had booked the Beattie for a steam test to see whether in the modern age, it would be feasible to run a steam locomotive through the tube's tunnels.

The tests were run from London Underground's Lillie Bridge depot in the early hours of Sunday, February 26 after the Tube closed for the night. It was seen mainly by orange-jacketed LU workers.

A TALE OF TWO ACTRESSES

Lillie Bridge is a place where history has been made.

In 1867, a sports ground was opened there. That year, it held the first-ever amateur boxing matches, with the Marquis of Queensbury providing the

first trophies and giving his name to the Queensbury Rules.

The ground also hosted hot-air balloon festivals and county fairs, and in 1873 hosted the second FA Cup final, which saw Wanderers successfully defend the cup by beating Oxford University 1-0. The low turnout of 3000 was blamed on the Boat Race taking place on the same day.

In 1876, Marshall Brooks set a world record of 6ft 2½in for the high jump, in front of a crowd of 12,000.

The ground was later superseded by Chelsea's Stamford Bridge and closed in 1887 following a riot in which the grandstand and track were destroyed.

Today, Lillie Bridge is best known as the site of the Earls Court Two exhibition centre and its Earls Court Two annexe, which is built above the railway lines that lead into London Underground's Lillie Bridge maintenance depot.

Near the entrance to the depot stands a pub named the Lillie Langtry, after the London actress and mistress of the future Edward VII.

However, for our trip through the tunnels, we were more concerned with another actress, *Sarah Siddons*, who lived a century before Lillie. The best-known Shakespearean tragedy actress of her day, her name was taken by the Metropolitan Railway's electric Bo-Bo locomotive No. 12.

Sarah Siddons was to accompany No. 30587 on its clandestine trip, connected to the smokebox end of the locomotive and used as passenger accommodation for the 18 guests who had been invited to witness the proceedings, including Peter Hendy, the commissioner of Transport for London, Leon Daniels, managing director of Surface Transport and Howard Collins, the chief operating officer of London Underground.

At the other end of the Beattie, a bogie permanent-way wagon was attached, with emergency supplies of Forest of Dean coal in blue sacks and water in giant plastic containers, which could be linked to the engine via a diesel pump if needed.

THE LEGENDARY BEATTIES

The legacy of the Beattie well tanks indeed predates that of the Metropolitan Railway, for it was in 1850 that it was decided that London suburban passenger services should be operated using small tank locomotives and mechanical engineer Joseph Beattie was ordered to produce designs.

Eventually, his Nile class of 1859 evolved into a standard design of 2-4-0WT, of which 85 were built between 1863 (when the Metropolitan Railway opened) and 1875.

The well tank handled heavy loads with speed and ease, but the success of the suburban services meant that they were soon replaced ▶

Stephenson Locomotive Society's 'South West Suburban Rail Tour' of December 2 and 6 that year.

After years on static display at Buckfastleigh, the National Collection-owned No. 30587 was restored to working order through a very generous sponsorship by retired London banker Alan Moore through the Bodmin & Wenford Railway Trust, and overhauled at the Flour Mill. The Moore-Parker team later also completed the restoration of sister No. 30585, which is based at the Buckinghamshire Railway Centre, home of No. 1.

INTO THE DARK

Going gingerly where no Beattie well tank had ever gone before, the special train left Lillie Bridge just after 1am and first ran to Kensington Olympia, where the platforms were deserted.

Reversing back to Earls Court and picking up the VIP guests who had been invited on the trip, including the author, the test train then took the District Line through Paddington.

Stopping momentarily at Edgware Road, it then followed the Circle Line route to its destination of Baker Street, a distance of around seven miles.

At Baker Street, the locomotive safety valves opened and blew off while heat and smoke levels in the station were tested. Photography apart, the well tank left proof of a brief presence in the form of soot rings on the roof of the tunnel.

by bigger and more powerful engines as passenger demand soared.

Most Beattie well tanks had been withdrawn by 1899, but three were transferred to the then-isolated LSWR's westernmost outpost of the Bodmin & Wadebridge railway in 1895.

For more than six decades, they became the engines that they couldn't scrap.

Earmarked for withdrawal on a number of occasions throughout the first half of the 21st century, it was found that no other types were as suitable for working the very tight curves of the Wenfordbridge line, and it was not until 1962 that the three were finally replaced by a trio of GWR 13XX pannier tanks.

LBSCR 'Terriers' apart, by then the Beattie well tanks were the oldest working locomotives on the British railways.

That year they returned home to London in style, with the two survivors, Nos. 30585 and 30587, taking a starring role in the Railway Correspondence & Travel Society/

The train, with the Beattie providing much of the power despite its sandwich position in the very unorthodox 'permanent way' working, then pulled forward into the tunnel and reversed back to the westbound platform, from which it ran a full-power test from Baker Street back to Edgware Road.

Meanwhile two standard tube trains, comprised of S stock and C77 stock, followed the steam train to test the effect, if any, that it had on them.

A WORKING BREAKFAST

Back at Edgware Road, the train made a two-hour breakfast stop, with guests being amply supplied with refreshments in the adjacent London Underground offices.

Our host was Sam Mullins, director of London Transport Museum, who outlined his plans for the 150th anniversary celebrations, while launching a £250,000 public appeal to cover the cost of the restoration of Met No.1, its major legacy project for the 2013 celebrations.

He highlighted the importance of the operation of heritage vehicles for members of the public to use and enjoy, and associated restoration projects as a means for young people to acquire workplace experience and new skills.

He announced that one of the guests, Phil Swallow, the majority shareholder in Severn Valley Railway-based rebuilt Bulleid West Country light Pacific No. 34027 *Taw Valley*, had handed over a cheque for £10,000 to kick-start the appeal, and there were promises from others that further sponsorship would follow suit.

A few guests left at Edgware Street, but most stayed on to return to Earls Court.

By the time the test train had returned to Earls Court shortly after 6am, the station was opening for Sunday services.

There followed what I will always remember as a 'Dr Who' moment.

As the engine came into view, it was as if a blue police box had suddenly materialised on the platform. A handful of startled waiting passengers were seen suddenly scurrying in their pockets for cameras because they could hardly believe what they were seeing and just had to capture it for posterity.

They knew only too well without photographic evidence, their mates would never believe their tale, perhaps thinking at best they had seen a ghost engine after downing a whisky or two.

ABOVE: Clear road ahead: a view of Lillie Bridge depot from the Beattie well tank's left-hand side cab window. ROBIN JONES

LEFT: The sign of the nearby Lillie Langtry pub. ROBIN JONES

ABOVE: Howard Collins, the chief operating officer of London Underground, and Peter Hendy, then the commissioner of Transport for London, and since July 2015 the chairman of Network Rail, with No. 30587 at Baker Street on February 26, 2012. ROBIN JONES

BELOW: No. 30587 stands in steam outside Lillie Bridge depot. ANDY BARR

ABOVE: No. 12 *Sarah Siddons* on shed at Lillie Bridge. ROBIN JONES

Apart from a unique trip through the tunnels, my lasting impression was of every one of the London Underground staff being hugely positive.

Even in comparison with heritage railways, which are run by people for love, I have rarely encountered staff who were not only passionate about their job, many enthusiasts themselves, but who were determined to ensure that the test steam trip was a roaring success. To millions of Londoners, the Underground is a functional fact of life, an everyday people mover, that makes the city work, but look beneath the surface, and it has a very human face indeed. ●

BELOW: Beattie well tank No. 30587 stands at Baker Street at around 2.20am on Sunday, February 26, 2012. ROBIN JONES

ABOVE: Steam running through Paddington's 'other' station, taken through the window of *Sarah Siddons*. ROBIN JONES

RIGHT: With no water supply available for steam locomotives on today's Underground system, the Flour Mill crew had to bring their own, carried on a maintenance wagon behind the well tank. ROBIN JONES

ABOVE: In more natural surroundings, Beattie well tank No. 30587 storms past a carpet of spring bluebells as it rounds Checkrail Curve on the Bodmin & Wenford Railway on May 3, 2014. GRAHAM NUTTALL

Chapter 11

From farm building to fame:
the phoenix co

One of the most remarkable successes of the Metropolitan Railway 150 celebrations was the restoration of sole-surviving 'Jubilee' carriage, No. 353, which spent several decades as a dwelling and then a farm building in Somerset. A real restoration rags to riches classic.

ABOVE: Immaculately restored Metropolitan Railway Jubilee carriage No. 353, an outstanding example of modern craftsmanship. ROBIN JONES

In 1892, the Sheffield coach-building firm, Cravens, built four-wheeled first-class carriage No. 353 for the Metropolitan Railway.

It was one of a type known as Jubilee carriages, because the first examples were constructed in 1887, the year of Queen Victoria's Golden Jubilee.

As the Metropolitan Railway empire grew, the Jubilee coaches were rendered obsolete as they were too small to cope with volumes of traffic.

In 1907, No. 353 was sold to the Weston, Clevedon & Portishead Railway, where it became the line's No. 12.

Built on the cheap under the 1896 Light Railways Act and opened a year later, this 13.8-mile line linked the three Somerset coastal towns in its name, running through sparsely populated countryside.

Typical of most standard gauge light railways, especially those that came into the Colonel Holman Stephens' empire (as this one did in 1911), most of the locomotives and rolling stock were bought second-hand from various sources, making a varied collection. Indeed, in this respect such lines were forerunners of today's heritage railways.

After years of financial struggle, the line was sold to the Great Western Railway and closed on May 18, 1940.

The GWR sold No. 12 for use by military tailors at Shrivenham in Wiltshire. The coach later became a US Army mess room

and after the war, it became used as a private dwelling and antiques shop, later becoming a farm building.

In 1974, the coach – also the sole-surviving vehicle from the Weston, Clevedon & Portishead Railway – was offered to London Transport Museum in part exchange for a platform seat. The museum kept it in unrestored condition, firstly at Syon Park and latterly at its Acton depot store.

In 2011, with the Metropolitan Railway 150 celebrations at the planning stage, the Heritage Lottery Fund agreed to finance the biggest share of an overall restoration package costing £572,000.

As well as the restoration of the coach itself, the project included an important skills transfer element, enabling apprentices to learn the skill of coach restoration and to transfer that practical knowledge to other restoration projects. The Friends of London Transport Museum group provided the rest of the cash.

In August that year, the coach body – its chassis having long since been scrapped – was taken to the Ffestiniog & Welsh Highland Railways' Boston Lodge works.

The contract was a major first for the works; the oldest in the world still in operation.

Widely acclaimed for its building both of new narrow gauge locomotives and replica original coaches, it was the first time that Boston Lodge had attempted a standard gauge project.

The first stage in the contract was widening the doors into the Boston Lodge carriage shop to enable the 4ft 8½in gauge vehicle to gain entry.

Over 15 months, the coach was rebuilt to original condition inside and out, and in mid-November 2012, was taken outside the historic works and mounted on the modified chassis of Southern Railway parcels van No. 1647. Craftsmen had worked round the clock to get it ready in time for Met 150.

ach!

ABOVE: The decayed body of Jubilee coach No. 353 inside London Transport Museum's Acton depot. LONDON TRANSPORT MUSEUM

ABOVE: Metropolitan Railway coach No. 353 ended up in use on a Shrivenham farm. LONDON TRANSPORT MUSEUM

ABOVE: A compartment of No. 353 being restored in meticulous detail at Boston Lodge. ROBIN JONES

ABOVE: Unique Metropolitan Railway Jubilee set survivor No. 353. ROBIN JONES

ABOVE: Ffestiniog & Welsh Highland Railway craftsmen worked round the clock to have No. 353 ready for Met 150. ROBIN JONES

The gleaming carriage, finished with gold leaf and carrying 12 coats of varnish on the exterior and nine on the inside woodwork, bore little resemblance to the sorry-looking hulk that had arrived at Porthmadog. However, 92% of the wooden frame is the original material.

More than half a mile of lining was applied to the outside as well as more than £700 worth of 23.5-carat gold leaf. There are no transfers on the carriage, as all signwriting was done by hand.

The carriage was originally fitted with gas lighting, forbidden under present safety regulations. Modern LED lamps have instead given the appearance of gas mantles to maintain authenticity.

"We will never be able to get a Mk.1 coach in the works, but we are proving that we can restore wooden-bodied vehicles for standard gauge lines to as-built condition, in every detail," said F&WHR general manager, Paul Lewin. "We hope that we will get more standard gauge carriage work as a result."

ABOVE: *Criccieth Castle* eases coach No. 353 across the Cob from Boston Lodge Works into Porthmadog. FR

ABOVE: When did you last enjoy luxury like this on a tube train? This is newly restored coach No. 353. FR

The carriage travelled from Boston Lodge Works and over Britannia Bridge in Porthmadog on November 16, 2012 behind diesel *Criccieth Castle*, a special chassis allowing it to be carried on 2ft gauge track, before it was loaded on to a lorry for onward transport to the Great Central Railway at Loughborough.

ABOVE: Everything on restored Met coach No. 353 was painted by hand. ANDREW THOMAS

ABOVE: The hand-painted Metropolitan Railway logo in coach No. 353. FR

ABOVE: Madam – your coach awaits. Yours too, sir! The luxury of restored Jubilee coach No. 353 has to be seen to be believed. FR

CARRYING WATER NOT MILK

A second Metropolitan Railway vehicle to be restored to take part in Met 150 was milk van No. 3.

Built in 1896 by the Birmingham Carriage & Wagon Company, it was designed to carry milk directly from dairy farms in Hertfordshire and Buckinghamshire into London.

The vans were attached to fast passenger trains and each carried many large churns of milk. They were ventilated to keep the milk fresh in transit and additional suspension was added so that it did not begin to turn into butter.

It ran on the Metropolitan Railway from 1896 to 1936 and was withdrawn from traffic in 1930. It later came into the London Transport Museum collection and was stored at its Acton depot.

Following its overhaul at Traincare's Wolverton depot, it undertook test runs on the Epping Ongar Railway, which was once part of the Underground network.

It was rostered for the Met 150 specials so that it could carry a back-up of supplied of water for the train's locomotive. ●

LEFT: Metropolitan Railway milk van No. 3 at Acton before its restoration. ROBIN JONES

London Underground S stock train models

London Transport Museum's new motorised 1:76 (OO) scale S stock model London Underground train is now available.

This is the first time a highly detailed 'ready to run' London Underground model train has been produced.

Manufactured exclusively for London Transport Museum by Bachmann Europe plc.

A motorised set comprising of 4 cars including 2 driving cars

☑ 35-990 DM Car   ☑ 35-990 M1 Car   ☑ 35-990 MS Car   ☑ 35-990 DM Car

Additional individual un-motorised cars may be purchased to authentically complete either S7 or S8 train formations

☐ 35-995 M2 Car   ☐ 35-996 MS Car   ☐ 35-995A M2 Car   ☐ 35-997 M1 Car

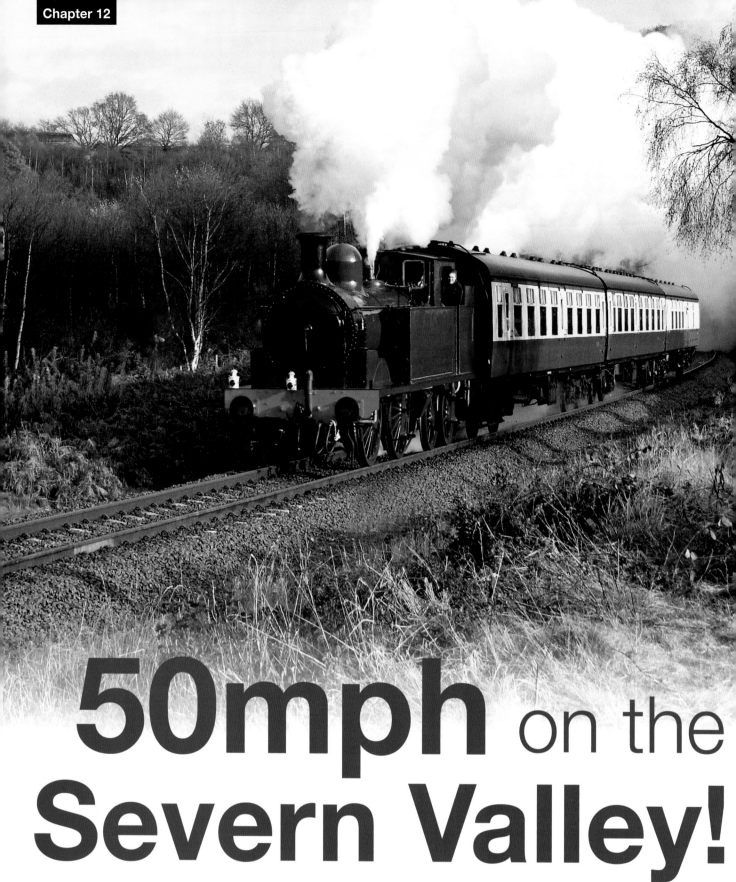

Chapter 12

50mph on the Severn Valley!

The Metropolitan Railway 150 celebrations may have taken place in the capital, but were by no means an all-London affair. Several heritage lines made their own key contributions to the ground-breaking event, not least of all the Severn Valley Railway, where the headline locomotive, Metropolitan Railway E class 0-4-4T No. 1, underwent a series of secret test runs at 50mph, twice the normal line speed.

ABOVE: The boiler of No. 1 (left) passed its hydraulic test at the Flour Mill workshops on July 16, 2012, as did that of Kerr Stuart 0-4-0 well tank No. 3063, supplied new to a Chepstow shipyard in 1918. Upon completion, the well tank became the Flour Mill's works shunter. BILL PARKER

ABOVE LEFT: Metropolitan Railway 0-4-4T No. 1 heads back towards Bewdley from Kidderminster at 25mph on November 30. PAUL CHANCELLOR

ABOVE: No. 1 fills the Flour Mill workshop with steam in November 2012. BILL PARKER

U nder the Light Railways Act of 1896, virtually all of today's heritage railways have a maximum speed limit of 25mph.

However, in order to qualify for a return to London Underground metals, Metropolitan Railway E class No. 1 had to be tested at twice that speed.

Its £250,000 overhaul was completed at the Flour Mill workshops on November 21, 2012, when it steamed outside, in unlined red livery.

Two days later, amid as much secrecy as practical, it arrived at Bitton near Bristol for three days of running in on the Avon Valley Railway, where teething problems were picked up and adjustments made.

No. 1 successfully undertook both light engine and loaded test runs with a rake of three maroon-liveried British Railways' Mk.1 coaches.

After that, No. 1 was moved to the Severn Valley Railway, Britain's second most popular heritage line in terms of visitor numbers.

However, there was nobody around to see the action that followed, as again a blanket of secrecy was imposed.

On the Severn Valley, more test runs were undertaken on November 28-29, with No. 1 hauling three Mk.1 carriages, painted in the carmine and cream livery of the Fifties.

Advantage was taken of the line's load weight apparatus to ensure that the wheels were properly balanced, and it was found that a slight adjustment had to be made.

BELOW: No. 1 in steam outside the Flour Mill workshop on November 21. ANDY BARR

ABOVE: Still unlined, No. 1 stands at Kidderminster in readiness for another loaded test run. ANDY BARR

Finally, on Friday, November 30, the much-anticipated high-speed runs took place.

Special dispensation for these runs had to be first obtained from the Office of Rail Regulation (since renamed the Office of Rail and Road) by the line's officials.

These trials were necessary because of the risks involved in running steam trains on the Underground between regular service trains carrying up to 1200 people.

Met 150 organisers had to be fully assured that the locomotive would cope in the intensive environment of today's tube.

Firstly, a run took place at 25mph, between Bewdley and Kidderminster, bunker first. The run was repeated at 35mph, then 40mph.

Finally, the moment of truth came, when No. 1 repeated the trip at 50mph – and passed all the tests with flying colours.

The high-speed runs were made on the eastbound leg of the journey, with the return trips, chimney first, all at 25mph.

Now it was all set for the Underground, and the final piece in the Met 150 jigsaw was complete.

The following Tuesday; December 4, No. 1 was back on home territory, having been taken by low-loader to Acton depot.

It was rostered to undertake a series of night-time test runs from Lillie Bridge depot

ABOVE: No. 1 stands ready for a loaded test run at Bitton on the Avon Valley Railway. ANDY BARR

ABOVE: No. 1 being moved into Acton depot on December 4, 2012, following its successful 50mph test runs on the Severn Valley Railway. ANDY BARR

to Earls Court and Baker Street early on December 16.

These trials followed on from the night-time tests involving LSWR Beattie well tank No. 30587, and were to involve *Sarah Siddons* and coach No. 353, as preparations for the first steam passenger journeys on the original stretch of the Metropolitan line since 1905 reached an advanced stage. ●

ABOVE: No. 1 raises a head of steam along the Avon Valley Railway. ANDY BARR

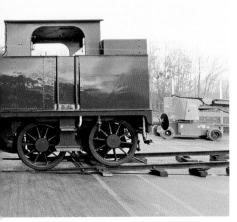

RIGHT: No. 1 inside Acton depot, in readiness for a series of night-time test runs through the tunnels. ANDY BARR

Chapter 13

Met 150:
the big one!

*The railway preservation movement has pulled off
many Mission Impossibles, since a band of volunteers
took over the ailing Talyllyn Railway in 1950. However, some
of its biggest global headlines were generated in early 2013
when the latest milestone saw the successful operation of a
complete fare-paying, passenger-carrying Victorian train with
teak coaches through the tube's tunnels beneath the streets
of the capital, in-between standard electric services.*

BELOW: Metropolitan Railway E class 0-4-4T No. 1 and its test train plough their way through driving snow at Edgware Road with a Met 150 special on January 20, 2013.
JOHN TITLOW

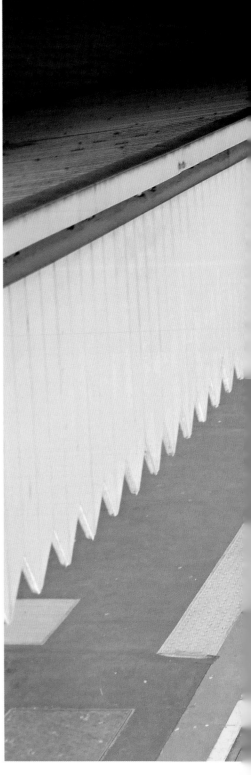

ABOVE: Proud Flour Mill driver Geoff Phelps checks over Met No. 1 at Moorgate. ROBIN JONES

The test runs using Beattie well tank No. 30585 proved that steam could indeed be run on today's London Underground tube systems without setting off fire alarms and contravening a raft of other safety measures.

The success of that run gave the green light both for the £250,000 overhaul of No. 1 and to make the unthinkable happen – a series of public steam trains over part of the District and Circle lines on Sundays January 13 and 20, running in-between modern tube services.

The big factor, however, which has made it all happen, was teamwork.

During the lengthy and secret preparations for Met 150, I viewed the concept in its finest hour, made possible by the sheer willingness of everyone at London Underground, from senior management right down to the orange-jacketed workers who populated the stations during the preliminary test runs.

Following night-time adventures below the city streets with the Beattie, the second and acid test run, involving Met No. 1, was also a closely guarded secret, and occurred shortly after 1am on Sunday, December 16.

After its 50mph test runs on the Severn Valley Railway, Metropolitan Railway

E class 0-4-4T No. 1 undertook a loaded test run from Ealing Common depot to Moorgate, but this time carrying around 30 VIP passengers.

Invited guests boarded original Met carriage No. 353, magnificently rebuilt from derelict to as-new condition at Boston Lodge Works at a cost of around £200,000, and which had completed its own test runs on the Great Central Railway.

Guests included mega-enthusiast Sir William McAlpine and his wife Judy, who have a private standard gauge railway and magnificent railway museum at their Fawley Hill home near Henley-on-Thames.

The test train consisted of Met No. 1, followed by No. 353, a low-sided wagon carrying spare containers of water and Bo-Bo electric No. 12 *Sarah Siddons* on the rear.

The purpose of this night-time trip was to identify any problems that might arise with steam operation so that they could be rectified before the public runs, and indeed there were lessons to be learned.

The test run took place during the hours when the tube is closed to the public, and followed part of the world's first underground railway route, which went from Paddington to Farringdon on January 9, 1863.

With Flour Mill driver, Geoff Phelps, having his hand on the regulator, the 2012 train also formed the first steam working through the King's Cross St Pancras Underground station and part of the new Farringdon station.

Water was taken on at a lengthy stop at Moorgate, from where *Sarah Siddons* propelled the train back.

Breakfast for those on board was provided at Edgware Road station around 3.30am. Guests left at either Edgware Road or Earls Court, after which the train returned to Ealing Common depot and the museum's Acton depot, where its huge collection of stock, not displayed at Covent Garden, is stored.

As the museum depot has no third-rail connection, No. 1 had to perform shunting duties to bring *Sarah Siddons* back inside, at around 5.30am.

ABOVE: Met No. 1, Jubilee coach No. 353 and *Sarah Siddons* in the platform at Edgware Road on December 16, 2012. JOHN TITLOW

BELOW: Still unlined, Met No. 1 coupled to its Jubilee coach No. 353 at the front stands at the Moorgate station bufferstops on December 16, 2012. ROBIN JONES

ABOVE: Among the VIP guests on the December 16 test run were mega-enthusiast Sir William McAlpine, honorary president of many of the UK's heritage lines, and his wife Judy. ROBIN JONES

ABOVE: Letting off steam at Moorgate. ROBIN JONES

LEFT: Taking on water at Moorgate station during the December 16, 2012 test run. ROBIN JONES

ABOVE: There are no water columns for steam engines on today's Underground. Therefore a special rail-mounted water tank for replenishing the tanks of Met No. 1, pictured at Moorgate, was constructed. ROBIN JONES

ABOVE: *Sarah Siddons* moved back into the depot by No. 1. ANDY BARR

ABOVE: Met No. 1 shunting at Acton depot after the December 16 test run. There are no electrified lines in the yard, so No. 1 had to shunt *Sarah Siddons*. ROBIN JONES

THE CHESHAM SET ARRIVES

ABOVE: The Bluebell Railway's Chesham set back on the Underground at Lillie Bridge depot. ANDY BARR

On Saturday January 5, 2013, the four wooden-bodied Ashbury coaches from the Bluebell Railway arrived by low-loader at Lillie Bridge depot.

When the Bluebell began operations in 1960, the cheapest coaches on the market were some ex-Metropolitan Railway ones, dating from the end of the Victorian era, for which London Transport wanted just £65 each.

Four of the six coaches, which had been used for the previous two decades as push-pull sets on the Metropolitan Line's Chesham branch before they, too, were displaced by electrification, came to the Bluebell. Another went to the London Transport Museum, and the sixth was scrapped.

In 1963, the four returned to the Underground to take part in the Metropolitan Railway's centenary celebrations, at which No. 1 played a starring role, and two of the carriages, Nos. 394 and 397 plus Met No. 1 were displayed at Rickmansworth during the final Steam on The Met event in May 2000.

Now, after agreement was reached with the Bluebell to hire them for this most special of events, they had returned to fulfil their original purpose to carry public passengers.

ABOVE: Still waiting to be lined, Met No. 1 is inspected at Acton depot on December 15, 2012. ANDY BARR

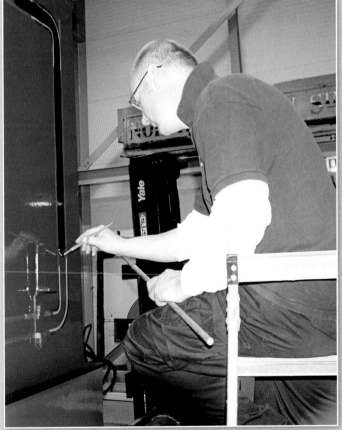

ABOVE: Met No. 1 being lined out at Acton depot in early January 2013. ANDY BARR

LEFT: The newly applied Metropolitan Railway crest on No. 1. ANDY BARR

ABOVE: At 2am on January 10, when the rest of the tube system has fallen silent and station doors everywhere are locked, Met No. 1 and its Victorian train heads though Baker Street station. JOHN TITLOW

THE FINAL TEST RUN

On Tuesday, January 9, during a stock movement involving Met No. 1, No. 353 and *Sarah Siddons*, a Piccadilly Line tube train kept up with the steam train for a considerable distance from Acton Town. The spirit of parallel running from the original Steam on the Met series had briefly returned!

Passengers on board the tube train were visibly astonished and many of them clamoured to take photographs of the steam train running alongside.

At a 'dress rehearsal' at 1am on Thursday, January 10, 2013, the completed train – Met No. 1; milk van No. 3; Jubilee coach No. 353 and the four-coach Chesham set, with vintage No. 12 *Sarah Siddons* again on the rear – and designated as an engineer's train - took around 75 passengers from Earls Court via Baker Street to Moorgate where it stopped for tests, before returning to Edgware Road and Earls Court by 4.15am.

It was the final precursor to the first of the history-making first public steam-hauled passenger trains on the Underground since 1905, three days later.

Two days of steam services were arranged, Sundays January 13 and 20. If all went well, more trips would follow…

ABOVE: No. 1 and No. 12 *Sarah Siddons* on shed at Lillie Bridge depot. ANDY BARR

BELOW: Standing at Moorgate with its final test train in the early hours of January 10, 2013, Met No. 1 displays a new pair of lamps. They were borrowed only the day before from new-build £3 million Peppercorn A1 Pacific No. 60163 *Tornado* especially for the Met 150 trips through the tunnels. The A1 Steam Locomotive Trust therefore became the latest in a line of heritage steam outfits that contributed to Met 150. ROBIN JONES

ABOVE: In-between the borrowed lamps above the bufferbeam a tiny video camera allows the crew to see the modern Underground signals on a viewing screen in the cab. ROBIN JONES

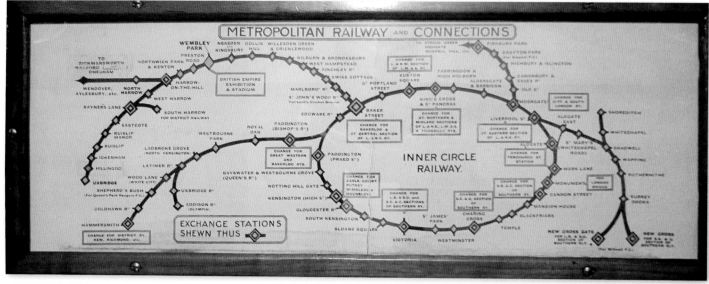

ABOVE: Original Metropolitan Railway system maps were displayed in several of the train carriages. ROBIN JONES

ABOVE: Standing on the pavement outside Edgware Road station is this immaculate 20th-century wooden police telephone box, pictured after the January 10, 2013 overnight test run. It brought back memories of the 1968 Dr Who serial The Web of Fear, which saw the Yeti robots take over much of London Underground. Over the next few days, there would be much travelling through time, as a train from the late Victorian era blended in with modern tube trains of 2013 during the Met 150 celebrations. ROBIN JONES

ABOVE: During a stock movement before the public steam specials, surprised tube passengers looked from the platform to see a steam train running almost parallel for a considerable distance. ANDY BARR

ABOVE: The footplate of Met No. 1 was the warmest place on the Underground on a bitterly cold January night! ROBIN JONES

RIGHT: Newly liveried and lined, Met No. 1 simmers alongside the platform at Edgware Road on January 10, 2013. ROBIN JONES

ABOVE: Ancient and modern stand together at Euston Square. JOHN TITLOW

THE VIP SPECIAL LAUNCHES THE SHOW

On Sunday, January 13, *Sarah Siddons* hauled the train from Lillie Bridge depot to Kensington Olympia, arriving at 10.44am.

The special departed from Kensington Olympia behind Met No. 1 at 10.54am, around 10 minutes later, taking 36 minutes to run non-stop to Moorgate.

Sarah Siddons was needed on the rear to haul the train back because there are no run-round facilities at Moorgate.

On the guest list were Mayor of London Boris Johnson, transport minister Patrick McLoughlin and under-secretary Stephen Hammond, along with Steve Shewmaker, president of Cubic Transportation Systems worldwide, the major sponsor of the Met 150 event.

ABOVE: The Metropolitan Railway 150 steam specials headboard. ROBIN JONES

ABOVE: London Underground chief operating officer, Howard Collins, with Met No. 1 at Kensington Olympia on January 13, 2013. He was one of those responsible for coming up with the idea of the Met 150 celebrations. ROBIN JONES

ABOVE: The Mayor of London Boris Johnson interviewed for the cameras before departure from Kensington Olympia. ROBIN JONES

ABOVE: Met No. 1 set to depart from Kensington Olympia with the VIP special on January 13, 2013. ROBIN JONES

ABOVE: Mirror image: a view in reverse of Met No. 1 at Kensington Olympia on January 13, 2013. ROBIN JONES

ABOVE: Headed by Met No. 1, the January 13, 2013 VIP special that opened the Met 150 celebrations heads away from Kensington Olympia. JAMES CORBEN

Also on the list were Roland Aurich from Siemens, another sponsor, and Keir Fitch, vice-president of the European Commission in charge of transport.

They were joined by Baron Adonis, secretary of state for transport from 2009-10, and Baron Tunnicliffe, chairman of London Underground and chief executive of London Regional Transport; both between 1998-2000, and Baron Faulkner of Worcester.

Also travelling were proud Flour Mill owner Bill Parker and Ffestiniog & Welsh Highland Railways' general manager Paul Lewin, whose staff at Boston Lodge had by then been universally praised for the rebuilding from derelict condition of No. 353.

Boris Johnson commented: "There is no other system as good as London Underground. It has inspired imitators around the planet."

Regarding the steam special, he said: "It was just extraordinary. We had steam coming in through the windows, huge thick clouds of white steam going past and then bits of soot coming through from the engine.

"As the train started to go up from Kensington to Notting Hill you could feel the engine really strain, but as we levelled off it picked up a lot of speed.

"You understand all those Victorian novels and the assignations that possibly took place on those velvet seats. It was pure Conan Doyle."

At Moorgate, actors and actresses in period costume greeted the VIP party, while driver Geoff Phelps was feted as a celebrity.

Afterwards, the 150-strong VIP party boarded a modern Underground train to King's Cross-St Pancras tube station, which is the biggest interchange station on the London Underground, serving six lines on four pairs of tracks as well as two national rail termini; it is served by more Underground lines than any other station on the network.

The first underground station at King's Cross opened as part of the original section of the Metropolitan Railway in 1863 and was rearranged in 1868 and 1926. The underground part of the station underwent extensive remodelling works to increase throughflow of passengers resulting from the opening of HS1/the Channel Tunnel Rail Link. The expanded station now has four entrances, and was completed in November 2009.

The VIPs enjoyed a buffet lunch in the Grand suite at St Pancras International before Boris Johnson gave a speech to mark the start of the Met 150 celebrations.

LEFT: Bill Parker, owner of the Flour Mill workshop, which played an integral part in Met 150, is interviewed by a journalist aboard the VIP special. ROBIN JONES

BELOW: We're off! The VIP special, the first of the Met 150 series of steam trains through the tube's tunnels, pulls away from Kensington Olympia on January 13, 2013. JOHN TITLOW

ABOVE: Smoke fills the London Underground tunnels during the run to Moorgate. ROBIN JONES

ABOVE: Ffestiniog & Welsh Highland Railway general manager, Paul Lewin, and Boris Johnson, seen in front of No. 1 at Moorgate on January 13, are clearly extremely well informed about railway heritage. *Heritage Railway* and *The Railway Magazine* were media partners with London Transport Museum for Met 150. ROBIN JONES

ABOVE: A flower seller and a Victorian lady greeted passengers at Moorgate station. ROBIN JONES

LEFT: Sir Peter Hendy, then transport commissioner for London, takes in a view of Moorgate station from the cab of Met No. 1. ROBIN JONES

ABOVE: Flour Mill driver Geoff Phelps talks to the world's media at Moorgate.
ROBIN JONES

ABOVE: Moorgate station is packed as crowds queue to glimpse the sight of a Victorian steam train in the platform on January 13, 2013. ROBIN JONES

THE PUBLIC JUMPS ON BOARD!

The public trips that followed in the wake of the VIP special also ran like clockwork.

Those riding on the train this time round paid between £150 and £180 per head to ride just 7½ miles behind steam, on what is a once-in-a-lifetime occasion, and one which, like the London 2012 Olympic Games, once again focused the eyes of the world on this great capital city.

So many people wanted to buy the tickets that a ballot had to be held.

Stories about the steam specials appeared within 24 hours across the globe including China, the US, India, Australia, Indonesia and Canada.

They reminded the world that Britain not only gave it the steam railway locomotive, changing the face of the globe

forever, but decades later invented the underground railway.

A normal tube service ran throughout the Sunday despite the presence of the steam specials. Proving that the ultra-modern Underground can still handle steam trains in the tunnels, might well be considered to deemed its finest hour yet.

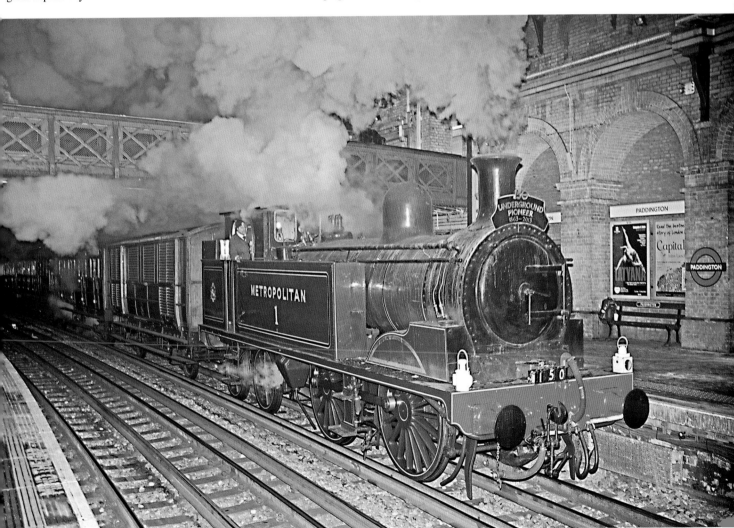

ABOVE: Met No. 1 storms through Paddington Underground station with a Met 150 special on January 20, 2013. JOHN TITLOW

ABOVE: Met No. 1 gets up to speed on an overground section of the Underground on January 13, 2013. JAMES MANSELL

British Transport Police and station staff were friendly and made announcements of the train's progress.

At King's Cross, an announcement warned travellers that a steam train was running and not to be alarmed if they saw smoke in the Underground!

At Euston Square, a station supervisor alerted people on one platform that a tube train was approaching and as it could stop you seeing the steam train, it might be best to change platforms.

When he was asked to hold the tube train so it would not spoil the view, the whole station roared with laughter!

ABOVE: London Underground posted notices telling onlookers how to behaving during the January 13 and 20, 2013 steam runs. ROBIN JONES

ABOVE: Eager photographers greet the arrival of a steam special at Moorgate, as seen from the cab of Met No. 1. ANDY BARR

LEFT: The right kind of snow for Met No. 1 and its Victorian teak train! ANDY BARR

ABOVE: London Underground chief operating officer, Howard Collins, with Met No. 1 at Kensington Olympia on January 13, 2013. He was one of those responsible for coming up with the idea of the Met 150 celebrations. ROBIN JONES

ABOVE: This Victorian gentleman at Moorgate station was one of several characters in period costume from 1860s. ROBIN JONES

ABOVE: The strong arm of the law: a British Transport Police officer stands shoulder to shoulder with a bobby from the days of Jack the Ripper on the bufferbeam of No. 1 at Moorgate. ROBIN JONES

The cost of staging Met 150 was a drop in the ocean compared with that of the London 2012 Olympics, and no, in this case the taxpayer was not asked for loose change to make up the cost.

London Transport Museum funded the cost

of the overhaul of Met No. 1 from its own charitable funds, and having raised £94,000 from a nationwide appeal through *Heritage Railway and The Railway Magazine*, did not need to draw on underwriting funds offered by Transport for London.

Despite the ticket prices, the trains were a sell-out. Around 65% of the 2200 available seats for the 10 evening steam runs on January 13 and the following Sunday were sold to the public, while 22% were allocated to Transport to London staff.

Around 13% went to sponsors, officials and partners in the project.

A THOROUGHLY BRITISH SUCCESS

ABOVE: The Met 150 planning team had by then defied all expectations, so a trifling matter of snow on the second public day of the steam trips, January 20, was no problem. ANDY BARR

It was the culmination of two years of dogged determination, hard slog and raw but genuine railway enthusiasm by the Underground's heritage rail operations manager Andy Barr and his team that made the once-unthinkable happen.

Yet Met 150 was not just about London and its Underground, but about the entire British preservation movement at its finest.

Heritage lines, which have no natural affinity with the capital, joined forces with London Transport Museum and Andy Barr's Underground heritage team to became part of the masterplan to

bring steam-hauled passenger trains back to the tunnels.

The Bodmin & Wenford Railway loaned Beattie well tank No. 30587 for the test runs; the Buckinghamshire Railway Centre signed a 10-year deal with the Covent Garden museum for Met No. 1 to be overhauled and not only used in the Met 150 trains, but hired out to other lines following its overhaul at the Flour Mill in the Forest of Dean.

We saw how Jubilee coach No. 353 was meticulously overhauled at Boston Lodge Works and tested on the Great Central Railway.

ABOVE: The team that made the impossible dream of steam-hauled passenger trains in the Underground tunnels happen after an absence of 108 years: test train operators Nick Kennet and Ian Blake, kneeling is Bill Parker (Flour Mill), Tim Shields (London Transport Museum), Mike Earley (test train manager), Graham Neil (principal rolling stock engineer), Tim Wade (chef de train), Rowan Milward (Bluebell Railway), Howard Collins (chief operating officer, London Underground), Andy Barr (heritage operations manager), Sir Peter Hendy CBE (then Commissioner of Transport for London), Mark Honeywood (test train engineer), Ray Knell (test train operator, beside Mark), Derek Smith (test train operator), Chris Holmes (rolling stock adviser), Dave Brabham (technical services manager). Standing on the buffer beam of Met No. 1 are fireman Oliver Furnell and driver Geoff Phelps. Sir Peter was presented with the headboard from the steam specials after the last run on January 20. LONDON UNDERGROUND

Just take a look inside the wonderful plush velvet recreated interiors of each compartment, and maybe compare it with the modern Royal Train – and then ask which one is really fit for the Queen?

The Avon Valley Railway was used for testing of Met No. 1, before it moved to the Severn Valley Railway where special dispensation was given to run it at speeds of up to 50mph, to show that if need be it was capable of keeping time in-between the regular tube services. As it happened, there was no need to worry on that score.

London Transport Museum's Met milk van No. 3 underwent trial running on the 'lost' part of the Underground, the Epping Ongar Railway.

All of these components came together from far and wide across England and Wales to produce what, in terms of both railway and London heritage, was an inspirational event enjoyed and admired by all.

It was not only a stunning success for London, but for Britain too.

London Transport Museum director, Sam Mullins, described the Met 150 opening steam runs as a huge success that clearly caught the public imagination.

"I cannot imagine how the event could have been made any better. Not only were the platforms full of railway enthusiasts taking pictures but also ordinary members of the public who had turned out to see the steam trains. When they went past many platforms, there was applause.

"Some people had astonished looks when suddenly a steam train came out of a tunnel, but they all ended up smiling.

"The event did something for London and Londoners as well. Hopefully it will renew interest in London's transport heritage." Indeed it did.

ROYAL VISIT FOR JUBILEE COACH

Following the huge acclaim given to the Met 150 celebrations, and in particular restored Jubilee coach No. 353, which may considered to be the jewel in the crown of the Victorian wooden-bodied train, it was given the royal seal of approval by Her Majesty the Queen.

At noon on Wednesday, March 20, 2013, in her first official engagement after a brief spell in hospital with a digestive problem, the monarch came to Baker Street station, along with the Duke of Edinburgh and the Duchess of Cambridge, to inspect the coach after it was specially parked in platform 5.

The occasion was yet another celebration of the London Underground's 150th anniversary. The station's main ticket hall was closed to commuters, who had to use side entrances, and Metropolitan Line trains did not stop at two platforms used to host the reception where the royal visitors met Underground workers.

Broadcaster Wesley Kerr, London chairman of the Heritage Lottery Fund, which financed the lion's share of No. 353's restoration, chatted to the royal party, saying: "I saw the carriage at the (London Transport Museum) depot at Acton and it was completely derelict. We just thought it should be reanimated. It's a wonderful way of reconnecting with history."

The royal party walked through its modern equivalent, one of LU's new S7 trains, which offers air conditioning for commuters and is being introduced on 40% of the network.

LEFT: The Queen inspects Metropolitan Railway coach No. 353 at Baker Street station on March 20, 2013. PRESS ASSOCIATION

ROYAL MAIL JOINS IN

On January 9, the exact date of the opening of the Metropolitan Railway between Paddington and Farringdon Street, Royal Mail issued a set of 10 special stamps, celebrating the 150th anniversary of the Underground.

The stamps show a timeline of the development of the London Underground from the first steam-driven Metropolitan line service to one of the most modern Jubilee line stations, Canada Wharf.

£1.28 — 1999 — JUBILEE LINE AT CANARY WHARF

2ND — 1863 — METROPOLITAN RAILWAY OPENS

1ST — 1911 — COMMUTE FROM THE SUBURBS

2ND — 1898 — TUNNELLING BELOW LONDON STREETS

1ST — 1934 — BOSTON MANOR ART DECO STATION

£1.28 — 1938 — CLASSIC ROLLING STOCK

ROYAL MAIL

The Queen unveiled a plaque, naming the train Queen Elizabeth II.

The station is also associated with 221B Baker Street, the home of famous fictional detective Sherlock Holmes.

Richard Hodder – an actor from the organisation Spectrum Drama – dressed as the sleuth complete with tweeds and a deerstalker hat, and caught the eye of the Queen who joked, "we've got the real thing," when she saw him.

Before leaving, the royal party were all given Oyster cards to mark their visit. The Duchess was given a badge reading 'baby on board' during her visit, which the mother-to-be placed on her jacket.

The Queen's first journey on the London Underground was in May 1939 when she was 13 years old, with her governess Marion Crawford and sister Princess Margaret.

Her previous visit to a tube station was in February 2010, when she travelled to Aldgate station to meet staff and view a memorial plaque dedicated to the seven people killed on the Underground during the July 7, 2005 terrorist bombings.

Before that, in 1969, she drove a train on the then-new Victoria Line.

ABOVE: The new S7 tube train officially was named by the Queen after herself at Baker Street as part of the Met 150 celebrations. ANDY BARR

MAPMAKER HONOURED BY MET 150

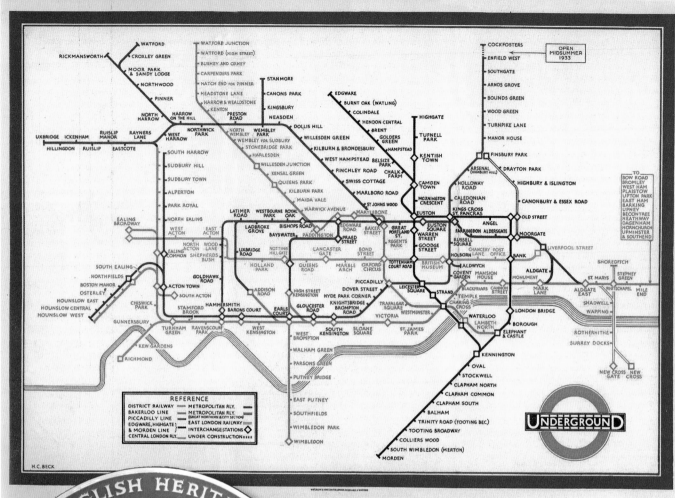

ENGLISH HERITAGE

HARRY BECK
1902 – 1974
Designer of the London
Underground map
was born here

Mike Ashworth, the design and heritage manager for London Underground, and blue plaque historian Howard Spencer gave speeches to mark the occasion.

Sam said: "Beck's map was revolutionary in its simplicity. It has become a London icon and influenced the design of many Metro maps across the globe, as well as being the inspiration for many contemporary artists and designers.

"His work forms part of the overall design ethic of Transport for London and its predecessor organisations, and his original artwork for the London map and the Paris Metro are both on display in London Transport Museum's Design for Travel gallery."

Mike Brown, managing director of London Underground, added: "Just like Harry Beck's map, the London Underground network is constantly evolving and improving to serve a growing population.

"The beauty and simplicity of Beck's design lends itself perfectly to the addition of new stations, new tube and rail extensions and new symbols for step-free access.

"It seems particularly fitting for English Heritage to have recognised Harry Beck's contribution to London Underground with a blue plaque during our 150th anniversary year."

In common with other English Heritage plaques to Underground-related figures, Frank Pick, Lord Ashfield and Edward Johnston, the inscription was set in the distinctive New Johnston typeface.

Beck was born in Leyton, the son of Joshua and Eleanor Beck, who had grown up in nearby West Ham. He would have spent about the first two years of his life living in a small terraced house in Wesley Road, which was then newly built.

By 1911 the Beck family had moved to Highgate, where Harry was educated at Grove House School. He attended art classes locally – where he met Nora, whom he married in 1933 – and also studied marble sculpture in Italy.

It is out of scale, out of shape and over simplified. Yet it is the world's best-known and probably most used railway map of all time.

And the Metropolitan Railway 150 celebrations saw that the man who designed London's tube map was honoured 80 years after the first version was published.

An English Heritage blue plaque was unveiled at 14 Wesley Road, Leyton, E10, birthplace of Harry Beck (1902-1974), by London Transport Museum director Sam Mullins on March 25, 2013.

SPRINGBOARD FOR SUCCESS... AND MORE STEAM

The phenomenal success of the Metropolitan Railway 150th anniversary celebrations undoubtedly raised the profile of the capital's world-beating transport system.

An all-out effort by all concerned, from the team led by London Underground's heritage operations manager to the superb staff in the public relations arm of London Transport Museum, reaped rich dividends, far greater than the initial investment.

The event switched the city public on big time to railway heritage. That was no more evident than on April 20-21, 2013, when nearly 6000 visitors turned up to London Transport Museum's Acton Depot open weekend.

The Ffestiniog Railway London-built George England 0-4-0TT No. 2 *Prince*, which dates from 1863, was celebrating 150 years since becoming the world's first narrow gauge steam line, gave short rides on a demonstration track, next to Metropolitan E class 0-4-4T No. 1 and restored saloon No. 353. The attendance was a record for the depot open weekend.

ABOVE: Harry Beck demonstrating his ground-breaking map. KEN GARLAND

By 1925, Beck had started working on a contract for London Transport as an engineering draughtsman in the London Underground signal engineers' office.

It was during one spell in between jobs, in 1931, that he produced his first design for a diagrammatic map.

Beck made the assumption that when travelling underground, overground geographic accuracy wasn't important and, after working on an electrical circuit diagram came up with the idea for his revolutionary new map, which was all straight lines and angles.

Beck continued to update the map as new stations and lines came into service.

Even after he left the employment of London Transport he still worked on the diagram; he is supposed to have been paid just five guineas for the original design. From 1947 he taught the history and theory of type and design at the London School of Printing.

Beck's last version of the map was published in 1960, after which a simmering dispute over its remodelling by other designers led to an unbridgeable rift with his former employers.

Despite this dispute, he continued to work on updated designs on his own, featuring the new Victoria Line a neat diagonal in lilac; these were never used, nor were the prototypes he produced for the Paris Metro map.

Beck was notably ahead of the game in producing a version of the London map showing all train services, underground and overground, as early as 1938, but then it was deemed too complex for publication.

Howard said: "Maps of transport systems in other cities owe a huge debt to Beck's icon of good design. Those of Moscow, Paris, Amsterdam and Singapore all use something of his simple, schematic approach.

"The London Underground map is essentially Harry Beck's sole claim to fame, but the impact it made on design practice and everyone who travels on the Underground cannot be underestimated."

However, a 2011 study suggested that 30% of passengers take longer routes owing to the out-of-scale distances on the tube map.

ABOVE: Met No. 1 lined up alongside Ffestiniog Railway's England 0-4-0TT No. 2 *Prince*, built in 1863, the same year as the first section of the Underground was opened, and one of the oldest steam locomotives in Britain currently in operation. ROBIN JONES

BELOW: No. 2 *Prince*, which was overhauled in time to celebrate its own 150th anniversary, was one of six narrow gauge steam locomotives built by George England & Co at its Hatcham Iron Works in New Cross, London. ROBIN JONES

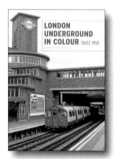

Chapter 14

Where no Great Western prairie has gone before!

The Flour Mill team won accolades far and wide, not only for the restoration of Metropolitan Railway E class 0-4-4T to the standard whereby it could once again haul timetabled underground passenger trains, but also for the professionalism of its locomotive crews. However, what if it could go one better – and bring a locomotive of its own to the Underground?

ABOVE: GWR small prairie No. 5521 makes a spirited departure from Wolsztyn during a main line test run on April 20, 2007, the year before it returned to Poland to haul regular timetabled passenger trains. MAREK CIESILSKI

Designed by GWR Chief Mechanical Engineer, Charles Collett, as a development of his predecessor George Jackson Churchward's 4500 class of 2-6-2T, the 4575 class, or 'small prairie' were small mixed-traffic locomotives, mainly used on branch lines.

Having larger side tanks and increased water capacity, 100 were built between 1927-29; numbered 4575-99 and 5500-74.

No. 5521 was built at Swindon in December 1927, and was to have a fairly run-of-the-mill career; first time round.

Allocated to Newton Abbot and then

Truro, it moved to Taunton in January 1930. Allocated initially to Bridgwater, in 1933 it was equipped with automatic staff-changing apparatus for working the Taunton to Minehead and Barnstaple routes.

In 1951, it briefly worked over the Cambrian Line from Oswestry, but that October it ►

ABOVE: When GWR small prairie No. 5521 was silently rusting away in Barry scrapyard, who would have thought that one day it would not only pilot the Venice Simplon-Orient-Express out of Budapest, but would head regular timetabled steam trips over London Underground? BILL PARKER

was transferred to St Blazey, from where it worked Par to Newquay passenger and freight trains. It also piloted heavy holiday express trains along that line.

No. 5521 also worked on the Bodmin Road-Wadebridge-Padstow line. Back at Taunton in August 1958, it worked Minehead and Chard branch trains, and ended up at Plymouth Laira, from where it was withdrawn in April 1952.

It arrived at the famous Woodham Brothers' scrapyard at Barry in September 1962, joining the long lines of main line locomotives rusting in the estuarial air by the Severn as they waited for the cutter's

torch. In the case of 213 steam locomotives bought from Barry for the preservation movement, that day never came.

The West Somerset Railway Association bought No. 5521, along with prairies Nos. 4561 and 5542, leaving Barry in September 1975. Nos. 4561 and 5542 were sold to repay the purchase debts and fund the restoration of No. 5521, which was bought by Bill Parker, he of Flour Mill fame, and his brother Richard, in 1980.

Its restoration began on the Dean Forest Railway, and when Bill reintroduced heritage engineering back in to the old

works at Swindon, as we have already seen, it was returned to its birthplace.

After Swindon Railway Workshop was forced to leave the site in 1992, No. 5521 moved to the nearby Swindon & Cricklade Railway, where it remained for some years under a protective sheet.

After Bill established the Flour Mill at Bream, No. 5521 moved there in 2001 so serious restoration could continue.

As the Bream locomotive repair business went from strength to strength, handling prestigious contracts for the National Railway Museum, the restoration of No. 5521 took very much a back seat.

However, on February 1, 2007, No. 5521 made the short journey by road from Bream to the nearby Dean Forest Railway, where it ran successfully under its own power the following day.

No. 5521 subsequently took part in the West Somerset Railways' 'Summer Saturdays in the West' spring steam gala, which broke all records by attracting 10,400 passengers.

However, it made its Minehead branch comeback with a decidedly continental appearance, as it had been fitted with an air brake allowing it to haul stock on the European main lines.

Why? Because No. 5521 had been booked to appear in the centenary celebrations being staged by Wolsztyn steam depot in Poland on April 28-29, 2007, and would be given the chance to haul special trains over that country's network.

Wolsztyn is the last bastion of European 'real' main line steam. A British enthusiast-led initiative, the Wolsztyn Experience, has helped finance the retention of the town's steam shed and its crews so that foreign visitors can be

LEFT: GWR No. 5521 and TKt No. 4818 double-head on the Polish main line. WOLSZTYN EXPERIENCE

BELOW: During a Polish main line test run on October 18, 2007, No. 5521 successfully hauled a single coach 20 miles from Wroclaw to Jelcz, and returned heading the Wolsztyn Experience's TKt 2-8-2 No. 4818 and two double-decker passenger coaches. The day was also Flour Mill engineer Geoff Phelps' birthday. THE FLOUR MILL

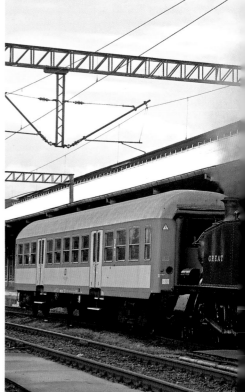

undertake steam-driver experience courses on a genuine, as opposed to preserved, main line.

The prairie was shipped from Hull to Poland via Helsinki, and took part in the parade alongside some of the finest preserved steam locomotives from Poland, Germany, Hungary and the Czech Republic. The Wolsztyn Experience organised a day-trip from Gatwick airport for enthusiasts wishing to attend the parade, and they were taken to Wolsztyn in a special train hauled by No. 5521.

After the centenary event, which included a parade of all the locomotives taking part, was over, No. 5521 was coupled behind Hungarian 4-6-0 No 109.109 – and the pair headed another enthusiast special, this time to Budapest.

There, No. 5521 went on display at the Hungarian National Railway Museum for the summer, and worked intermittently with MAV Nosztalgia, that country's heritage rail operator.

In September 2007 No. 5521 piloted the Venice Simplon-Orient-Express from Budapest Keleti to Kelenfold on its return from Istanbul to Venice.

It then competed in the Zvolen Steam Locomotive Grand Prix in Slovakia and the Central European Steam Locomotive Grand Prix at the Railway Heritage Park in Budapest. ▶

ABOVE: GWR prairie No. 5521 heads a demonstration freight on the Bodmin & Wenford Railway in 2010. OLIVER RIDGE

The Heritage Railway Association's annual awards in 2007 saw the Flour Mill presented with the John Coiley Award for locomotive projects for the restoration of GWR 2-6-2T No. 5521 allowing it, and its support team, to successfully act as an ambassador for British heritage engineering on its momentous journey across Europe.

No. 5521 returned to Poland and in May 2008 again appeared in the parade before hauling real suburban services from Wroclaw to Jelcz-Laskowice, to the timings of the electric multiple units it was replacing, for several periods of up to nine days at a time, each with 36 scheduled stops and starts.

In 2009, No. 5521 returned to England after appearing at the parade for the third time. It subsequently visited the Bodmin & Wenford, Dean Forest, Avon Valley, Swindon & Cricklade and the Battlefield Line railways.

The prairie had a Westinghouse air pump added on the driver's side, so that it has, along with a hand brake and a steam brake, the ability to haul trains fitted with both vacuum and air brake systems. A true go-anywhere GWR prairie!

After the success of the inaugural Met 150 runs through the tunnels in January 2013, Bill and his team began wondering – could No. 5521 yet again go where no class member had ever ventured before, and haul passenger trains on the Underground?

Clearly, at that stage, the tube tunnels were a non-starter, because of the height of its cab, but the Underground surface routes selected for steam specials later that summer

ABOVE: In Brunswick green livery, award-winning GWR 2-6-2T No. 5521 is displayed on the turntable in the Great Hall at the National Railway Museum in York on June 30, 2009. As it had run in service on the main line in Poland, it displayed a PKP (Polish State Railways) badge on its chimney. STEPHEN GILLETT*

were a different matter, as a GWR small prairie would comply with its clearances.

No prairie had hauled passenger trains over the Underground before, so this would be yet another 'first' for No. 5521.

London Underground requested that the locomotive be renumbered L150 and repainted into London Transport maroon livery, just like its pannier predecessors, to commemorate the 150th anniversary.

Furthermore, London Transport Museum commissioned Bachman Europe to design the livery and also produce an OO gauge model of the locomotive in it.

The Flour Mill carried out work on the locomotive in the spring of 2013, just in time for the operations.

Once consigned to the scrapyard, this Cinderella locomotive was now revelling in being the star of the ball! ●

BELOW: Running on a GWR branch in which it saw service in the steam era, No. 5521 hauls a service train past Charlie's Gate on the Bodmin & Wenford Railway. BWR

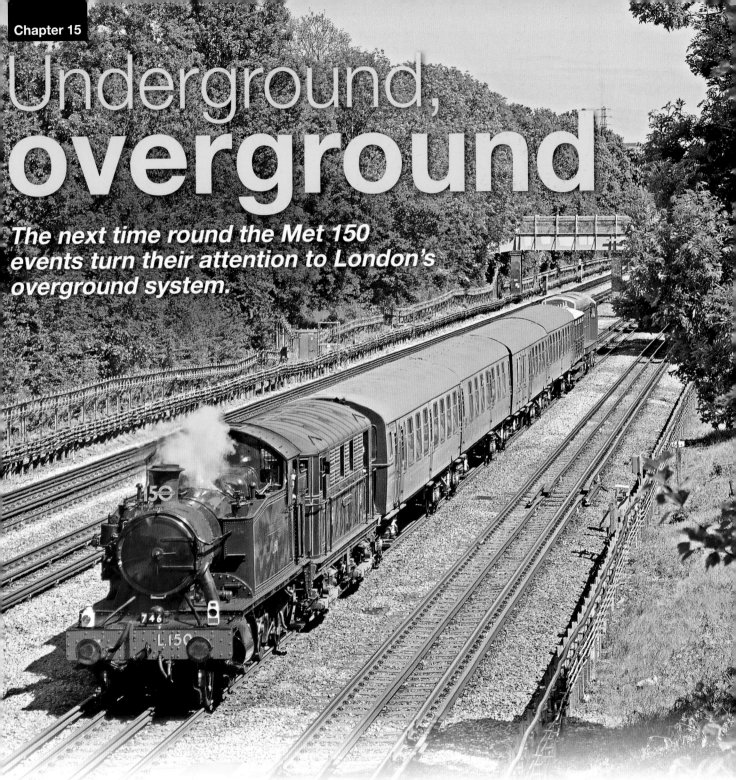

Chapter 15

Underground, overground

The next time round the Met 150 events turn their attention to London's overground system.

ABOVE: GWR prairie L150 (5521) heads between Northwood Hills and Pinner en route to Amersham on May 27, 2013. JOHN TITLOW

The phenomenal success of the inaugural Met 150 steam trains in the tunnels below the city streets was quickly followed up on the surface routes that run from the urban areas into the country fringes, and which also contributed to a major national award for London Transport Museum and its partner in the event, London Underground.

The Metropolitan Railway 150 celebrations were by no means exclusively about steam trains running through the tunnels beneath London.

Indeed, out of 250 route miles on the Underground, only about 45% are in tunnels.

While the Underground is predominantly an urban system – only five London Underground stations lie outside the M25 motorway – it still services country towns such as Amersham, which at 482ft above sea level, has the highest station on the system, as well as Chesham.

Following the stupendous success of the January 2013 specials, further events were arranged for the Met 150 year, including more steam specials but this time on Underground surface routes.

Entering the fray alongside Met No. 1 for these was not only Bill Parker's maroon-liveried GWR pannier L150 (5521), but also a pannier tank.

However, the organisers did not book one of the surviving 57XXs panniers that had worked for London Transport, but the sole-surviving operational 94XX, No. 9466, star of the first Steam on the Met event back in 1899, as highlighted in Chapter 8.

Now, as history repeated itself, it was again scheduled to rejoin Quainton Road stablemate Met No. 1, in the thick of the resumed Met 150 action over the Spring Bank Holiday weekend in late May 2013.

STEAM BACK ON THE MET

This time round, the public runs would not use the Bluebell Railway's Chesham set, but London Underground's own scumbled-finish ex-BR 4TC set with, of course, Jubilee coach No. 353.

On Friday May 24, No. 9466 hauled a special train for local school children between Wembley Park (first train of the day only), Harrow-on-the-Hill and Amersham, while another private service was run for Underground staff under the banner of the 'Howard Collins'.

The three days of public running effectively consisted of three non-stop 50mph round trips, two complete ones and another two one-way.

The start of the proceedings was delayed by around an hour owing to a track possession in Ruislip depot, but no matter: the time was made up and the final service of the day ran to the timetable.

ABOVE: Red prairie L150 heads through North Harrow with an empty stock working on May 27, 2013. JOHN TITLOW

ABOVE: GWR 2-6-2T L150 (5521) and Met No. 1 at Ruislip depot on the evening of May 25, 2013. ANDY BARR

Met 1, together with vintage Met Bo-Bo electric No. 12 *Sarah Siddons* and LT-liveried Class 20 No. 20189, ran a test train from Ruislip depot via Harrow to Amersham after midnight on May 23.

As stated, preparations for both the underground and above-ground steam trips were carried out with meticulous precision, leaving no stone unturned; but with locomotives ancient and modern, there can always be a glitch on the day.

As it was, on Saturday, May 25, one of the motion bearings on Met No.1 ran hot during its first trip. To avoid any chance of causing serious damage, the locomotive was withdrawn from traffic – and in stepped L150, which had been delivered to Ruislip depot only three days before.

Bill Parker's engine gave immaculate service during the rest of the series, running the trips as planned in top-and-tail mode with three visiting privately owned Class 20 diesels, two of which, Nos. 20189 and 20227 had been repainted in versions of London Underground livery and the other, No. 20142, in British Rail corporate blue with double-arrow logo. Again, they were backed up by No. 12 *Sarah Siddons*.

No Class 20s in such liveries had even been seen in Underground service before.

The idea of painting a classic main line engine in a livery that its type never carried in the steam era at one stage would automatically provoke howls of derision from hardcore linesiders.

However, this time round, the idea of a red prairie was not only meant to mark the Metropolitan Railway's historic links with the GWR, dating back from its start in 1863, but also as pure and simple fun – and it worked spectacularly.

Virtually all of the 220 seats on each train, top price £45, were sold out. On the first round trip from Amersham to Harrow and back on the Saturday, guests were surprised by an appearance by TV celebrity chefs the Hairy Bikers, Simon 'Si' King and Dave Myers, who were recording material for a new show aboard the train, and handed out Chelsea buns to passengers.

The duo had earlier been to Ruislip depot and King could not praise the organisers of the event enough.

After the event, Bill Parker and Flour Mill workshop driver Geoff Phelps, who had driven L150 throughout, took the big end from Met No. 1 and headed back to base at Bream in the Forest of Dean. There, the component was to

ABOVE LEFT AND RIGHT: For the 'surface' runs of the Steam Back on the Met steam specials, three privately owned Class 20 diesels were hired to provide support, primarily running the trains in top-and-tail mode, and two of them were repainted into London Transport-style colours, No. 20189 in maroon and No. 20227 in red, white and silver. The other was No. 20142, which was carrying British Rail corporate blue.

BELOW: Hawksworth pannier No. 9466 enters Amersham with the 'Howard Collins', one of the private specials on Friday, May 24, 2013. ANDY BARR

ABOVE: Never a London Transport pannier, but a British Railways 94XX, No. 9422 is seen shunting new 1959 tube stock into London Underground's Ruislip depot from the British Railways' main line on March 11, 1960, so there was a slender historical precedent for No. 9466's appearance in Steam Back on the Met. Match wagons and a brake van form part of the train. HK NOLAN/TFL, LONDON TRANSPORT MUSEUM COLLECTION

ABOVE: The May 27, 2013 empty stock working between Harrow-on-the-Hill and Ruislip depot. JOHN TITLOW

ABOVE: Hairy Bikers Dave Myers and Simon King aboard a May 25, 2013 return trip from Amersham to Harrow-on-the-Hill. ROBIN JONES

be remetalled and returned to Ruislip without delay, for refitting.

No. 1 returned to action for its star visit to the Epping Ongar Railway for two gala weekends in late June.

ABOVE: Western Region 0-6-0PT No. 9466 with Class 20s Nos. 20227 and 20142, which formed part of the Steam Back on the Met fleet, were used to run trains in top-and-tail mode. ANDY BARR

BELOW: Met No. 1, pannier No. 9466 and No. 12 *Sarah Siddons* stand at Amersham with the coaching set for the specials on May 25. ROBIN JONES

ABOVE: L150 (left) with Met No. 1 double-heading with No. 9466 during shunting movements at Amersham on May 25, 2013. ROBIN JONES

BELOW: Prairie L150, No. 12 *Sarah Siddons* and the 4TC coaching set at Ruislip depot, waiting to depart. ANDY BARR

ABOVE: London Transport-liveried Class 20 No. 20189 takes one of the special trains through Chorleywood station to Harrow-on-the-Hill on May 25, with the red prairie on the back. ROBIN JONES

BLACK PANNIER REIGNS SUPREME ON THE MET

The Steam Back on the Met runs were reprised in early September 2013.

On Saturday, September 7, two public round trips and two private charters ran; one for London Underground staff and one for VIPs attending the London conference of global public transport organisation UITP.

The following day, four public trips were run. The Sunday services were linked to free vintage bus services from Amersham to Old Amersham for a special heritage day at the town's museum, with free entry for train ticket holders.

All went as planned on the Saturday, with the trio ably backed by LT-liveried Class 20s No. 20189 and 20227.

However, on the Sunday, only the 94XX appeared. Such was the demanding regime that has been imposed on the running of Met trips after an absence of many years that no chances were taken when faults were detected with the other two locomotives.

No. 1 was found to have a tiny steam leak from its tube plate, and so failed its fitness-to-run examination at Ruislip depot in the morning.

The expert team from the Flour Mill workshops at Bream, which had overhauled the locomotive, arrived and had the problem fixed inside five minutes.

Sadly, it was too late as by then, the roster had been readjusted.

Woe befell L150 when it too failed, in this instance with boiler tube leaks, following a summer in service on the Bluebell Railway and its new and hugely successful northern extension to East Grinstead.

However, No. 9466 performed in style throughout the rest of proceedings, emphasising its power with the final train of the day, when it completed a storming run up the grade from Harrow without any diesel assistance whatsoever.

ABOVE: Frames by the iconic overhead cable frame in the former goods yard at Chorleywood, No. 9466 heads a September 8, 2013 special to Amersham with Class 20s No. 20189 and 20227 in tow. PETER FOSTER

ABOVE: Met No. 1 hauls the 4TC coaching set with a Class 20 diesel on either end at speed through Moor Park on September 7, 2013. JOHN TITLOW

ABOVE: Hero of the hour: on September 8, 2013, as in 1971, a pannier tank again comprised the only steam on the Underground. ANDY BARR

ABOVE: Met No. 1 gleaming in the morning sunshine at Harrow-on-the-Hill. ANDY BARR

ABOVE: Right on time, Western Region 0-6-0PT No. 9466 brings the first train of the day, from Wembley Park via Harrow-on-the-Hill, into Amersham at 10.59am on Sunday, September 8, 2013. ROBIN JONES

ABOVE: The end of a hard day's work: the smokebox of No. 9466 liberally filled with clinker! ANDY BARR

ABOVE: Met No. 1 and its train at Amersham on September 8, 2013. ANDY BARR

THE LORD MAYOR'S SHOW

In recognition of the historical importance of the opening of the first section of the Metropolitan Railway in 1863, the honour of becoming the first railway vehicle to be 'cart marked' was bestowed on Jubilee coach No. 353 during the summer of 2013.

The London tradition of cart marking, traditionally reserved for road vehicles, dates back more than 500 years when all carts and carriages plying trade within the Square Mile had to be licensed to operate within the city limits. The licence took the form of a branded mark applied directly to the vehicle.

Organised by the Worshipful Company of Carmen, a livery company of the City of London, the ceremony usually involves marking a vehicle with a branding iron and takes place in the forecourt of the Guildhall.

The 'road vehicles only' tradition was departed as a one-off in recognition of the 150th anniversary of the London Underground, the role of the City of London in the financing and building of the Metropolitan Railway, and the essential role that underground travel plays in the life of the city.

As the vehicle could not get inside the Guildhall forecourt, Alderman Fiona Woolf CBE, the prospective Lord Mayor of the City of London, and the Master Carman, Neil Coles, took a branded plaque, prepared earlier at the Guildhall, to the carriage at Mansion House station on Wednesday, July 17.

The carriage had been taken there from Earls Court station sandwiched between a pair of London Underground battery locomotives. It stood for several hours on platform 2 for public examination before the ceremony was carried out.

London's then Transport Commissioner Sir Peter Hendy CBE, a member of the Worshipful Company of Carmen, said: "The City of London played a crucial role in lobbying for and funding London's first underground railway, the Metropolitan Railway, and has been consistent ever since in supporting better transport in order to develop the capital's economy.

"The extension of this ancient ceremony with the London Transport Museum's finely restored Victorian carriage of the Metropolitan

ABOVE: Pictured with the newly branded coach No. 353, displaying its 483 cart mark, left to right, are London's then Transport Commissioner Sir Peter Hendy CBE, Master Carman Neil Coles, Alderman Fiona Woolf CBE and Mike Brown, the managing director of London Underground. ANDY BARR

ABOVE: London Transport Museum director Sam Mullins, with No. 353 as it took part in the Lord Mayor's Show. ANDY BARR

Railway in the 150th anniversary year of London Underground highlights this connection."

For No. 353, it got better.

The coach was invited to part in the Lord Mayor's Show on November 9 that year.

As the oldest Underground carriage still in use, it was invited to join the annual spectacle in the capital's streets – rather than be pulled below them – to mark the 150th anniversary of the world's oldest subway line.

The coach was seen by an estimated half a million people who lined the streets to glimpse the pageant.

A float carrying the carriage and its passengers, which included Underground staff and representatives from the charities the Railway Children and London Transport Museum, joined a carnival of horses and carts, marching bands, vintage cars, giant robots, helicopters, tractors, penny farthings and the magnificent Gold State Coach belonging to the Mayor and aldermen.

Mike Brown MVO, managing director of London Underground and London Rail, said: "The Tube has always played an important role in the economic development of the London and UK economy so it seems fitting that we should take part in a festival in one of the world's major financial centres.

ABOVE: No. 353 travelled along the streets of London, not below them, in the Lord Mayor's Show procession on November 9, 2013. ANDY BARR

"We've supported Railway Children for many years. Sharing a float with the charity at the Lord Mayor's Show is an excellent way to highlight how the organisation is helping to transform the lives of children living on the streets."

The Railway Children charity works with children who live on the streets in India, East Africa and the UK. It aims to reach street children as soon as possible, keeping them safe, getting them home and saving them from a life on the streets.

ALDWYCH STATION 'REOPENS' FOR INTERACTIVE COMMUTERS

The Underground's disused Aldwych station was reopened for eight weeks to stage a unique interactive sound and light experience as part of the Met 150 celebrations.

London Transport Museum partnered Nexus Interactive Arts to develop the new 'immersive experience' in the Grade II listed station, which has not seen passengers since 1994.

The show, Lost and Found – a Secret Underground journey, reimagined the 150-year history of London's Underground through interactive installations, set design, moving image, sound and light.

Visitors were taken on an hour-long journey through the ticket hall and down on to the platforms during an experience that told the fascinating stories of forgotten characters, people and places.

The site-responsive set design meant that visitors were able to become a part of the story as it unfolded before them, making it a truly immersive experience.

The 75-minute production was launched on August 30, 2013, and ran for an eight-week period.

Situated close to the junction of Strand and Surrey Street, Aldwych was originally opened as Strand in 1907 as the terminus and only station on the short Piccadilly line branch from Holborn that was a relic of the merger of two railway schemes.

During its lifetime, the branch was the subject of a number of unrealised extension proposals that would have seen the tunnels through the station extended southwards, usually with the aim of reaching Waterloo.

Disused parts of the station and the running tunnels were used during both world wars to shelter artworks from London's public galleries and museums from bombing.

With low passenger numbers, the station and branch were considered for closure several times. A weekday peak hours-only service survived until closure in 1994, when the cost of replacing the lifts was considered too high.

ABOVE: A tube train at Aldwych station in 1958. TRANSPORT FOR LONDON

RIGHT: The exterior of Aldwych station in 1932. TRANSPORT FOR LONDON

▶

MET 150 – THE JUDGES' CHOICE

The return of a complete passenger-carrying wooden-bodied Victorian steam train to the London Underground tunnels and a year of sell-out events to mark the 150th anniversary of the Metropolitan Railway led to the capital's transport museum being recommended for the top honour in the annual Heritage Railway Association awards.

The HRA, the successor to the Association of Railway Preservation Societies, is the umbrella organisation that represents Britain's heritage lines and museum venues.

At a meeting of the judges' panel at the National Railway Museum in York on November 20, it was agreed that London Transport Museum, London Underground and their partners should be recommended for the Peter Manisty Award for Excellence 2013.

The award was bestowed for the achievements and exhaustive programme of events to mark the 150th anniversary of the world's first underground railway including the successful operation of the train.

The 'partners' included the heritage railways which had contributed to two years of planning and preparation for the Met 150 celebrations.

ABOVE: The presentation of the Heritage Railway Association's Peter Manisty Award for Excellence by the organisation's president Lord Faulkner of Worcester to London Underground and London Transport Museum for the Metropolitan Railway 150 celebrations took place at the Guildhall in Bath on February 8, following a civic reception in the Roman baths the previous evening. Pictured left to right are the former Commissioner of Transport for London Sir Peter Hendy, London Underground technical services manager Dave Brabham, museum director Sam Mullins, Lord Faulkner and London Underground's heritage operations manager Andy Barr. GWYNN JONES

ABOVE: The Peter Manisty Award for Excellence 2013 plaque takes pride of place at the entrance to the main exhibit hall of the London Transport Museum in Covent Garden. ROBIN JONES

MET 1 MEETS THE SUPERCAR

At the Acton depot open weekend during Met 150 year, held during November 1-3, 2013, Met No. 1 was positioned alongside the 'Supercar'.

This very unorthodox bus was the product of a 1991 TV campaign jointly funded by Network SouthEast and London Transport to promote one-day travelcards following the change of brand name from Capitalcard two years earlier.

With a 'Superman' theme, the advertising agency Gold Greenlees Trott came up with the concept of 'Supercar'.

Former London bus DMS 1515 Daimler Fleetline/MCW, registration THM 515M, was purchased from South Yorkshire Passenger Transport Executive and converted into a unique bus, tube and NSE Class 321 'omni-vehicle' capable of running on both road and rail.

The conversion was undertaken by John Maher of Pine Films.

After the filming of the Supercar TV commercial the vehicle subsequently appeared in the Lord Mayor's Show, the Bus of Yesteryear Rally and Southend airshow in 1992.

As seen on its destination board, it is now used by the Epping Ongar Railway for publicity work as well as touring bus and vintage transport shows.

ABOVE: Met 1 alongside the bus/tube/train 'Supercar' at Acton on November 3, 2013. LONDON TRANSPORT MUSEUM

ABOVE: L150 and *Sarah Siddons* double-head the 3.05pm special to Uxbridge out of Harrow-on-the-Hill, running in parallel with a modern tube train. ROBIN JONES

A NEW STEAM CLASS ON THE UNDERGROUND!

More capital railway history was made on Sunday, December 8, 2013 when L150 – headed a series of six special public trips from Harrow-on-the-Hill to Uxbridge.

However, unlike its long-scrapped sister locomotives, the prairie was not running to the former GWR terminus at Uxbridge, which was closed half a century ago, but the town's Underground station.

L150 was chosen to head the last of the Met 150 year steam specials.

Its appearance on the six 40-minute non-stop round trips was made after short notice, following the failure of Met No. 1 with an ancient steam leak, which chose to burst forth as a repair dating back 60 years gave out.

After Met No. 1 completed a test run from Ruislip depot to Uxbridge on December 3, it was noticed that steam was escaping from the concrete base beneath the locomotive's smokebox.

Andy Barr, London Underground's head of heritage operations, said that at first it was thought that a blastpipe gasket was leaking. The steam escaped only when the regulator was opened, and it was feared that a blowback might occur.

An area of the concrete was needle-gunned out piece by piece and at the top of the steam chest, it was discovered that there was a very old copper patch repair measuring about six by five inches that had started to leak.

Andy feared that detritus from the concrete could find its way into the steam chest and eventually into the pistons, scouring them and causing severe damage.

A decision was therefore taken on the Friday afternoon before the Uxbridge runs to fail No. 1, and request L150 to be brought back from the Flour Mill.

L150 indeed came – but not as anyone had ever seen it before.

As the go-anywhere GWR small prairie and its crew had impressed everyone with their dazzling performances, it was prepared to go where no member of its class had ever gone before: inside the Underground tunnels!

While second-hand GWR pannier tanks were used on freight and works trains by London Transport from the mid-Fifties until 1971, no prairie ever ventured inside the tunnels because of the loading gauge.

RIGHT: The ancient copper patch repair of No.1's steam chest undertaken by London Transport decades ago had finally given out. ANDY BARR

BELOW: Metropolitan Railway No. 1 stands inside Uxbridge station during its December 3, 2013 test run. ANDY BARR

ABOVE: A driver's eye view of Metropolitan Railway No. 1 approaching Ruislip on its December 3, 2013 test run. ANDY BARR

ABOVE: Pictured in the Flour Mill workshop, GWR small prairie No. 5521 (L150) becomes the first of its class to be fitted with a cut-down cab so it can run through the tube's tunnels. BILL PARKER

However, the Flour Mill workshop had spent the previous weeks building an alternative cab for L150, with lowered roof, so it could clear the tunnels.

The new cab allowed L150 to run anywhere on the Underground sub-surface lines apart from the deep tubes on potential future trips. From then on, it was able to run between Ruislip depot and London Transport Museum's Acton depot, and indeed could from then on go anywhere where Met No. 1 could.

Bill Parker noted that because of the modification the locomotive was now a sub class of the GWR small prairie type.

As it also hauled trains carrying fare-paying passengers, it could also be considered as the 'new' last steam locomotive type in Underground service.

Again, the first locomotives on the Underground were GWR types, and on the Uxbridge trips, L150, which afterwards was booked to make a second visit to the Bluebell Railway, performed faultlessly. Tucked in behind it on the outward journey was No. 12 *Sarah Siddons*, the 4TC set and No. 353. At the far end was BR blue-livered Class 20 No. 20142, running in top-and-tail mode because of the lack of run-round loops on the system.

All six trips were packed, and linesiders again congregated at every vantage point in the glorious sunshine to watch and photograph the specials, which also marked the centenary of Uxbridge station in advance of the 2014 anniversary.

ABOVE: The new lower cab fitted to L150 in the Flour Mill workshop. BILL PARKER

The Harrow & Uxbridge Railway, which later became part of the Metropolitan Railway, first opened a station in Uxbridge on July 4, 1904. The first station stood in Belmont Road, a short distance to the north of the present station, and was situated on a different track alignment, now used as sidings.

The original service from central London was provided by steam-hauled trains with electrification taking place in 1905.

The current station was opened on December 4, 1938.

Uxbridge High Street station, which was sited in what is now Oxford Road, was the southern terminus and the only station on the short GWR Uxbridge branch from the GWR/GCR joint line, now the Chiltern Main Line.

The High Street station opened on May 1, 1907, and closed to passengers as early as September 25, 1939. Freight continued until the station closed completely in July 1964 during the Beeching era.

Regarding the leaking gasket, which had prevented Met No. 1 from reaching Uxbridge on anything other than a December 3 test train, Andy Barr said: "It was a problem that nobody who had overhauled the locomotive in preservation could have spotted. The path repair was likely to have been carried out by London Transport in the Sixties, or even as long ago as the Fifties."

However, now that the ancient patch repair had been identified, rectification was a relatively straightforward task and No. 1 was soon ready for service again.

ABOVE: The 10.50am hauled by L150 from Harrow-on-the-Hill approaching Rayners Lane station at the junction with the Piccadilly Line on December 8, 2013. JOHN TITLOW

ABOVE: The 3.50pm empty coaching stock moves back from Harrow to Ruislip depot headed by L150. JOHN TITLOW

ABOVE: The London Underground and Flour Mill team that ran the Uxbridge specials. LONDON UNDERGROUND

LEFT: GWR prairie No. L150 inside Uxbridge station on December 8. ANDY BARR

'BRIGHTEST LONDON' WINS SIEMENS' POSTER CONTEST

As part of the Met 150 celebrations, London Transport Museum held an exhibition titled Poster Art 150 – London Underground's Greatest Designs.

A total of 150 classic tube posters were on display, and visitors to the museum were asked to vote for their favourites.

More than 42,000 people voted in the Siemens Poster Vote, so named after the principal Met 150 sponsor.

The public decided that the best London Underground poster of all time was Brightest London is best reached by Underground, designed by Horace Taylor in 1924.

Brightest London drew 1752 of the votes, with London Zoo by Abram Games (1976) and Underground – the way for all by Alfred France (1911), 1614 and 1342 votes respectively.

The winning poster was created when cinemas still showed black and white films; however, vibrant posters such as this splashed colour into Twenties London.

Taylor presented the Underground as bright, popular and extremely fashionable with a very smart crowd heading out for a night on the town.

Still vibrant almost 90 years after it first appeared to brighten Underground stations, it is easy to imagine how effective it must have been at the time.

The artist's granddaughter once explained that Taylor often liked to paint himself into his

ABOVE LEFT: London Zoo by Abram Games.
ESTATE OF ABRAM GAMES & TRANSPORT FOR LONDON
ABOVE RIGHT: Underground – the Way for All.
TRANSPORT FOR LONDON

posters. In this one he is the gentleman with the top hat and the beard on the middle escalator.

The Poster Art 150 exhibition opened on February 15, 2013 and was due to close in October but its popularity meant it was extended until January 5.

The posters were selected from the Covent Garden museum's archive of more than 3300 Underground posters by a panel of experts; the 150 that appeared in the exhibition show the range and depth of the museum's collection.

Siemens Rail Systems UK managing director, Steve Scrimshaw, said at the time: "We were proud to be part of the 150th anniversary of London Underground, and have been delighted

ABOVE: Brightest London is best reached by Underground.
TRANSPORT FOR LONDON

by the success of the Siemens Poster Vote – it has really captured people's imaginations."

The judges included Tamsin Dillon, London Underground's head of art, Catherine Flood, a prints curator in the word and image department at the Victoria and Albert Museum, Oliver Green, research fellow and former head curator at London Transport Museum, contemporary artist Simon Patterson, Dr Paul Rennie, a senior academic at Central Saint Martins, Nicolette Tomkinson, a Christie's director and head of its vintage poster department, Michael Walton, head of trading at London Transport Museum, and Brian Webb, a designer and visiting professor at the University of the Arts, London.

MUSEUM LAUNCHES EXCLUSIVE PATRONS CIRCLE CLUB

In the wake of the success of Met 150 celebrations and the resulting huge upsurge in public interest in the capital's transport heritage, London Transport Museum launched an exclusive club to fund similar events.

The new £2000-a year Patrons Circle was launched at a private event on Monday, January 27, 2013.

To mark the launch, the museum's four-coach 1938 tube stock set ran a special trip for invited guests from Tower Hill station clockwise around, appropriately, the Circle Line to King's Cross St Pancras station, where a reception addressed by museum director Sam Mullins was held.

To join the club, patrons must donate at least £2000 a year, which will go towards funding museum projects. In return, they get preferential tickets to special events and a special annual programme of exclusive behind-the-scenes events including access to parts of the transport system closed to the general public.

These events include tours of disused stations – as well as overnight 'steam' test events, such as those run in the build-up to the Met 150 runs.

Membership also gives free entry to the museum for patrons and their guests, invitations to private views and opportunities to meet the curators.

Anyone who would like to join is invited contact the museum's development team by emailing development@ltmuseum.co.uk or telephoning 0207 565 7442.

RIGHT: London Transport Museum's beautiful art deco special 1938 stock four-car set at Tower Hill tube station on January 27. ROBIN JONES

As another Met 150 spin-off, a time capsule marking the year of celebrations and made from a salvaged District line signalling box was displayed in the revamped Tottenham Court Road station.

To be opened in 2063, the capsule contains a letter from London Underground managing director Mike Brown to his future successor, a specially made short film showing a 'day in the life' on the tube in 2013, copies of the Evening Standard and Metro newspapers, a special-edition 150th anniversary Oyster card and a book charting the first 150 years of London Underground's history. ●

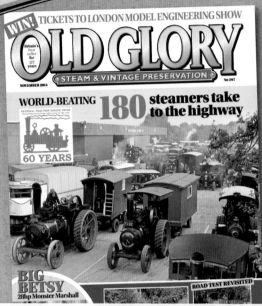

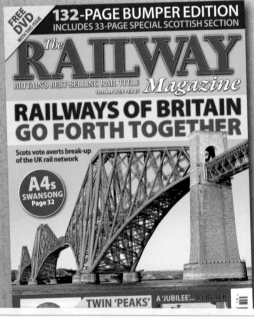
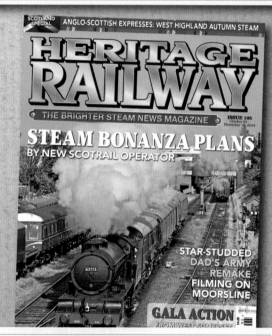

Chapter 16

Hammersmith & City 150

Following up from the national award-winning Metropolitan Railway 150 celebrations in 2013, fare-paying steam on the Underground was back the following August, after heritage trains manager Andy Barr and his team had shown it could be done. The first of the new series of trips celebrated the 150th anniversary of the Hammersmith & City Railway.

Following the rip-roaring success of the Metropolitan Railway celebrations, which began with public steam trains beneath the streets of the capital in January 2013, Steam on the Underground was back with a vengeance in 2014.

How many other subway systems are capable of running revenue-earning heritage steam trains in-between standard electric services in the middle of the day?

It appears that turning back the clock for a few days only serves to reinforce the status of London Underground as not only the most advanced system of its kind in the world but far and away the most versatile.

London was a very different place when the Hammersmith & City Railway opened on June 13, 1864.

The Hammersmith line was constructed on a viaduct over what were then mainly open fields. You would never have guessed that today.

As with the Metropolitan Railway in 1863, the GWR ran the initial services from Farringdon to Hammersmith. The Met ran the trains to Hammersmith from 1865, and in 1867 both companies took joint control of the line.

The Hammersmith & City was extended east of Farringdon to a new terminus at Aldgate on November 18, 1876. It was electrified in 1906.

BELOW: Metropolitan Railway E class 0-4-4T No. 1 at Farringdon with a Hammersmith & City 150 special to Moorgate on August 9, 2014. BRIAN SHARPE

BELOW: No. 1 emerges from Clerkenwell tunnel into the sunshine as it approaches Farringdon on August 9. BRIAN SHARPE

The 2014 steam runs held to mark the 150th anniversary of the line were staged on Saturday, August 2 and 9.

Each day, the first journey ran steam hauled between Northfields station on the Heathrow branch of the Piccadilly Line, and Moorgate, behind Metropolitan Railway E class 0-4-4T No. 1.

The next three journeys ran from Moorgate to Hammersmith behind No. 12 *Sarah Siddons*, returning to Moorgate behind No. 1.

The last run of each day saw *Sarah Siddons* haul the train from Moorgate to Northfields with No. 1 on the back of the train.

Just as with the Met 150 celebrations, the train again comprised Metropolitan milk van No. 5, the Bluebell Railway's four-coach Chesham set and the beautifully restored Metropolitan Jubilee carriage No. 353. At Moorgate, re-enactors and a brass band again greeted passengers.

The train ran non-stop, but at every station, a platoon of photographers was ready to savour the moment to the full.

What I found particularly remarkable was the large number of photographers from ethnic communities, a phenomenon I have never witnessed in the heritage sector before.

I have always found it to be the case that enthusiasts overwhelmingly favour their own country's railway heritage. Indeed, I have seldom seen visitors from ethnic groups in large numbers other than the occasional family unit at UK heritage lines.

The Underground steam runs, however, told a different story. London is one of the world's greatest multi-ethnic communities, and people from all walks of life turned out to record for posterity something different and magic that was happening on 'their' railway.

Over the past decades, we have heard much about multiculturalism and its

ABOVE: Met No. 1 undergoes final checks at Northfields depot on August 2, 2014. ANDY BARR

successes and failures. However, without even trying, it seems that London Transport Museum and London Underground are streets ahead – or rather below – in this respect.

During the event, steam seemed to me to become a great common denominator between people from many diverse backgrounds, all sharing a common interest. In this respect

alone, Steam on the Underground has been a brilliant success.

For people from all walks of life who regard the Tube as an everyday experience hardly worth thinking about, the appearance of steam trains running between electric ones is mind-blowing, and when the opportunity presents itself, it just has to be seen. ●

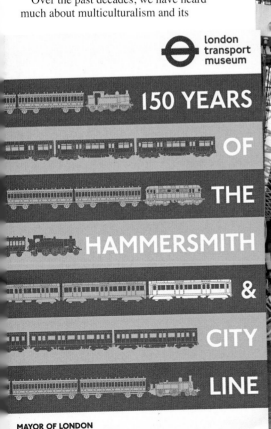

ABOVE: Raring to go: Met No. 1 comes off shed at Northfields depot on August 2, 2014. ANDY BARR

RIGHT: No. 1 and its all-steam Victorian train stands at Hammersmith station with the first round trip of August 2. ROBIN JONES

BELOW: Metropolitan Railway A class No. 4 *Mercury* in 1868 stands at the head of a four-coach set at the original Hammersmith station. LONDON TRANSPORT MUSEUM

BELOW: The first Hammersmith & City 150 special off Northfields shed on August 2, 2014, departs Earls Court. JOHN TITLOW

BARBICAN STATION

Barbican station was opened on the Moorgate extension from Farringdon as Aldersgate Street on December 23, 1865. The station replaced an earlier building at 134 Aldersgate Street, which for many years had a sign claiming, 'This was Shakespeare's House'.

Although the building was very close to the nearby Fortune Playhouse, there is no documentary evidence that Shakespeare lived there; a subsidy roll from 1598 shows a 'William Shakespeare' as the owner of the property, but there is nothing to confirm that it was the playwright.

On December 16, 1866, three passengers were killed, a guard was seriously injured and one other person suffered shock when a girder collapsed on to a passenger train in the station.

The name was shortened to Aldersgate on November 1, 1910 and it was renamed again on October 24, 1924 as Aldersgate & Barbican. Services were disrupted during the Second World War when the station suffered severe bomb damage in the Blitz, particularly in December 1940. This led to the removal of the upper floors and in 1955 the remainder of the street-level building was also demolished. On December 1, 1968, the name was simplified to Barbican.

Met No. 1 is seen heading through with a Hammersmith & City 150 special to Moorgate on August 9, 2014. BRIAN SHARPE

LEFT: No. 1 approaches Paddington from Hammersmith, alongside the Great Western main line on August 9. BRIAN SHARPE

BELOW: The Hammersmith & City Railway working timetable of July 1, 1864, issued by the GWR. LONDON TRANSPORT MUSEUM

ABOVE: West Kensington station is passed as No. 1 heads to Moorgate with a Hammersmith & City 150 special to Moorgate on August 9, 2014. BRIAN SHARPE

ABOVE: No. 1 ready to depart from Hammersmith on August 2, 2014. ROBIN JONES

BELOW: Amid the mesh of wiring that is a feature of the modern Underground, No. 1 heads its Victorian train backed by Bo-Bo electric No. 12 *Sarah Siddons* past Royal Oak. BRIAN SHARPE

ABOVE: A brass band greeted the VIP guests at Moorgate – a different take on the standard London street buskers! ROBIN JONES

ABOVE: A Victorian lady, policeman and flower seller greet passengers at Moorgate on August 9. ROBIN JONES

ABOVE: The cab monitor attached to a bufferbeam-mounted camera to assist steam locomotive crews in looking ahead when approaching signalled junctions, to prevent steam obscuring the vision of signals. ANDY BARR

ABOVE: Metropolitan Railway 0-4-4T No. 1 pauses at Baker Street during a late-night test run on July 29 before the first Hammersmith & City Line specials. JOHN TITLOW

ABOVE: No fast food takeaway above the ground for him! Flour Mill driver Geoff Phelps cooks breakfast in the time-honoured steam locoman's way during a pause in the Hammersmith & City 150 proceedings. ROBIN JONES

RIGHT: The combined group of test train operators, engineering and operating staff, with the footplate crew from the Flour Mill, Northfields Depot and the Bluebell Railway with Metropolitan Railway No.1 stands ready at Northfields for entry into service on the Hammersmith and Moorgate service. ANDY BARR

ABOVE: Metropolitan Bo-Bo electric No. 12 *Sarah Siddons* brings up the rear of the train as it departs from Hammersmith. ROBIN JONES

Chapter 17

Steaming back to
Chesham

Running past woodland and green pastures, Chesham offers sweeping views of the Chess Valley countryside.

Following the Hammersmith & City outings, two days of steam trips were held to celebrate the 125th anniversary of the Chesham branch.

The first trip of each day was one-way from Wembley Park to Rickmansworth, steam hauled.

The next trips were returns from Rickmansworth to Chesham, topped and tailed by steam.

The last trip ran from Rickmansworth to Chesham, returning to Harrow-on-the-Hill, again steam hauled in both directions.

The Chesham branch holds a special place in steam folklore, for it was here that the last timetabled London Underground steam-hauled passenger services were run. Four of the wooden-bodied coaches sold to the embryonic Bluebell Railway as soon as they were displaced by electric stock.

Inviting comparisons with the Epping to Ongar branch that London Underground closed in 1994, no part of the 3.89-mile Chesham branch is in London, or even in a suburban area.

By way of dramatic contrast, it runs through a wholly rural area, offering sweeping views of the rolling countryside of the Chess Valley.

The branch leaves the Metropolitan Line and the Chiltern Railways, route to Aylesbury at a ▶

BELOW: No. 1 approaches the summit of the 1-in-66 climb from Chesham towards the junction south of Amersham on August 16. BRIAN SHARPE

ABOVE: GWR prairie L150 at Ruislip depot alongside modern tube stock on August 16, 2004. ANDY BARR

junction at Chalfont & Latimer.

Chesham station, which still has its steam-age brick water tower intact but non-operational has, since 1961, been the westernmost point on the Underground network and since 1994 been the northernmost point too.

The branch, which opened in 1889, was built as part of Great Central Railway pioneer Edward Watkin's scheme to turn his Metropolitan Railway into a direct rail route between London and Manchester, but plans to extend the line north of Chesham to meet the LNWR never materialised.

In 1933, the Metropolitan Railway became part of London Underground, which viewed the rural routes in Buckinghamshire as an expensive anachronism.

So the day-to-day operation of the Chesham branch was switched to the LNER, while still controlled by London Transport.

Electrification of the Metropolitan Railway had begun in the wake of the 1903 appointment of Robert Selbie as secretary, but it was not started on the Rickmansworth to Amersham and Chesham section until 1957.

Electric T Stock began running to Chesham and Chalfont & Latimer on August 16, 1960.

As far as the public timetable was concerned, the last London Transport steam passenger train on the branch left Chesham at 12.11am on September 12, 1960. By then, average Sunday patronage had shrunk to around 100, but on this occasion, 1917 passengers used the line.

The day before, descendants of the Chesham residents who had attended Watkin's original meeting to promote the branch, along with 86-year-old Albert Wilcox, who had attended the opening of the line itself, travelled on the steam shuttle to Chalfont & Latimer and back before attending a ceremony in Chesham's council chamber.

Despite the ending of steam-hauled passenger trains, a steam locomotive was kept on standby in the new second platform at Chesham, as reserve in case the electric trains broke down.

While September 12, 1960 saw the last scheduled steam passenger service on the line, a British Railways' steam train continued to depart from Marylebone for Chesham each morning at 3.55am to deliver newspapers, returning as the first passenger train from Chesham at 5.58am. Not listed in the timetable, that service was open for public use but remained unadvertised, and lasted until June 18, 1962.

The final steam-powered passenger services on LT's remaining non-electrified section between Amersham and Aylesbury ran on September 9, 1961. After that, the line west of Amersham was transferred to British Railways, and A Stock replaced the T Stock from June of that year.

Steam would make a final appearance at Chesham in the Sixties. A former GWR 57XX pannier tank, now in London Transport maroon livery, arrived at the head of a demolition train in 1966, when the track in Chesham's goods yard was lifted. The newspaper service, by then run using diesel multiple units, ended on October 17, 1967, along with BR's presence on the branch.

It was therefore somewhat ironic that a GWR locomotive, also in London Transport maroon livery, led the August 16-17 special into Chesham, with Bill Parker's repainted GWR

ABOVE: L150 hauls the first special of the day into Wembley Park on Saturday, August 16, 2014. ROBIN JONES

WEMBLEY PARK

L150 gets the green flag at Wembley Park. When the Metropolitan Railway opened its extension from Willesden Green to Harrow-on-the-Hill in 1880, Wembley was a small rural hamlet not considered important enough to warrant a station of its own.

However, Metropolitan Railway chairman Edward Watkin – the same who later pioneered the Great Central Railway's London extension from Annesley north of Nottingham to Marylebone, saw a business opportunity at Wembley.

In 1881 he bought large tracts of land close to the railway and began a massive scheme to build an amusement park at Wembley, laid out with boating lakes, a waterfall, ornamental gardens and cricket and football pitches.

The centrepiece of this park was to be a soaring metal tower, known as Watkin's Tower; at 1200ft it was to be taller than the similarly designed Eiffel Tower and would offer panoramic views of the surrounding countryside, just 12 minutes from Baker Street station.

Wembley Park station was specially constructed to serve these pleasure grounds as a destination for excursion trips on the company's trains.

The station opened for the first time on October 14, 1893 and initially operated to serve only Saturday football matches in the park. It opened fully on May 12, 1894.

Watkin confidently anticipated that large crowds would flock to the park and the station design incorporated additional platforms to handle large passenger numbers.

Watkin's Tower ran into structural and financial difficulty; it was never completed and the partially built structure was demolished in 1904. Despite this, Wembley Park itself remained a popular attraction and flourished. ROBIN JONES

RIGHT: The modern entrance to Wembley Park station resembles the terraces of the famous football stadium. ROBIN JONES

ABOVE: Prairie L150 and its wooden-bodied train pulls into Rickmansworth on August 16, 2014. ROBIN JONES

small prairie No. 5521 chosen to lead because of its greater power, backed by *Sarah Siddons*, and No. 1 at the far end, there to haul the train back to Rickmansworth and, for the last service of each day, to Harrow-on-the-Hill.

As with Epping-Ongar, the Chesham branch faced closure because it generated little income.

In 1982, doubts as to its future were raised when it became clear that two bridges were deteriorating badly, leading to a 15mph speed restriction.

However, in one of its final acts before abolition, the Greater London Council, which had subsidised services, saved the day with a grant of £1,180,000 to replace the bridges.

Chesham had already seen steam in the heritage era.

The centenary of the branch had been celebrated in 1989 with steam specials over two weekends in July between Chesham and Watford, with packed trains and stations thronged with crowds.

As we saw earlier, the event proved so

successful that London Transport ran its much-loved Steam on the Met event annually until 2000, with Amersham mostly used as the terminus.

Incidentally, initial plans for the Crossrail scheme envisaged using the Chesham branch as a terminus.

HAPPY HOMECOMING

It was also fitting that the stock hired for the 2014 steam runs comprised four of the original coaches from the branch.

ABOVE: L150 calls at Rickmansworth on the first leg of its journey to Chesham on August 16, 2014. ROBIN JONES

ABOVE: No. 1 heads out of Rickmansworth towards Amersham and Chesham. Its train included the Bluebell Railway's coaches, which previously ran on the Chesham branch until they were displaced by electrification. ROBIN JONES

RIGHT: The approach to Chesham as seen from the footplate of L150. ANDY BARR

When they became redundant following the cessation of steam shuttles, LT offered them for sale at just £65 each.

The Bluebell Railway had started services in 1960 with just a pair of Southern Railway coaches, and so bought four of the six in use on the branch. Another went to the London Transport Museum, and the sixth was scrapped.

The Bluebell four comprises three Ashbury coaches, No. 394, built in 1900 as a seven-compartment third, No. 387, built in 1898 as a brake third, composite No. 368 built in 1898, and composite No. 412, built by Cravens in 1900.

From 1906 onwards, the 50 coaches supplied to the Metropolitan Railway were converted to electric multiple unit use.

Age took its toll and by 1938 all had been withdrawn but wartime shortages meant that in 1940 five were converted back for steam haulage along with an 1899-built experimental electric motor coach for use in push-pull sets on the Chesham branch.

In 1963, the Bluebell coaches made a comeback to the Underground to take part in the Metropolitan Line's centenary celebrations.

Later, the Chesham coaches were also withdrawn from Bluebell traffic as doubts for their survival were expressed.

However, in 2007, the successful completion of a marathon 16-year restoration programme, which saw them back in service almost as new, was recognised with the presentation to the railway of the Heritage Railway Association's Carriage & Wagon Award and The Railway Magazine Lamp. ●

▶

RIGHT: GWR prairie L150 at Chalfont with one of the Chesham specials on August 16, 2014. BRIAN SHARPE

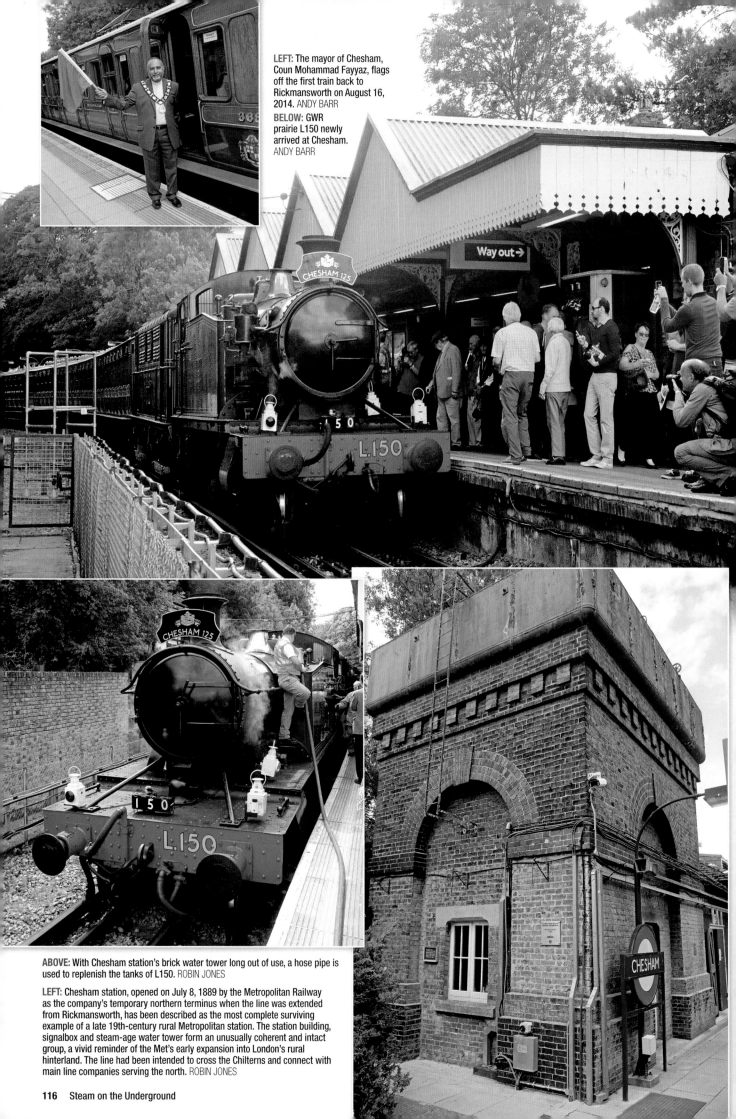

LEFT: The mayor of Chesham, Coun Mohammad Fayyaz, flags off the first train back to Rickmansworth on August 16, 2014. ANDY BARR

BELOW: GWR prairie L150 newly arrived at Chesham. ANDY BARR

ABOVE: With Chesham station's brick water tower long out of use, a hose pipe is used to replenish the tanks of L150. ROBIN JONES

LEFT: Chesham station, opened on July 8, 1889 by the Metropolitan Railway as the company's temporary northern terminus when the line was extended from Rickmansworth, has been described as the most complete surviving example of a late 19th-century rural Metropolitan station. The station building, signalbox and steam-age water tower form an unusually coherent and intact group, a vivid reminder of the Met's early expansion into London's rural hinterland. The line had been intended to cross the Chilterns and connect with main line companies serving the north. ROBIN JONES

ABOVE: A Class 165 DMU is seen calling on August 16, 2014. ROBIN JONES

RICKMANSWORTH WATER TOWER

Until 1961, Rickmansworth station was the changeover point from steam to electric locomotives for Metropolitan Line trains from Aylesbury and Verney Junction to London. The last regular steam services were withdrawn on September 10, 1961, The electrification was then extended north to Amersham and Chesham, leaving Aylesbury services to be served by Class 115 diesel multiple units, since replaced by Chiltern Railways' Class 165 and Class 168 units. Locomotive-hauled trains (steam and electric) on the Metropolitan line were then replaced by the new trains of A60 and A62 tube stock. However, its water tower survives intact, albeit disused.

Rickmansworth is still the changeover point for drivers on the Metropolitan line. The majority of tube trains heading north to Amersham are timetabled to stop at Rickmansworth for about five minutes to change train staff. It is also the headquarters of the operational side of the northern section of the Metropolitan Line. It controls signals on the line from Northwood in the south to Watford and Chorleywood in the north and is one of the few locations on the Met where train drivers are based.

BATTLE BUS

Despite the success of the August trips, which again required a phenomenal input in both arranging and running them, the primary focus of London Transport Museum for 2014 was not railways, but the Year of the Bus.

Over the weekend of September 13-14, the museum's Acton depot and its vast collections store again opened to the public, this time focusing on the role of London's Transport in the First World War.

The highlight of the open weekend was the appearance of the museum's 1914-built B-type bus No. 2737, which has been retro-converted to First World War condition, with khaki livery and boarded-up windows, ready to transport troops to the front line.

After the event, it was driven on a commemorative tour to the battlefields of northern France and Belgium including Arras, Passchendaele and Zonnebeke near Ypres, to commemorate the sacrifices made by transport workers during the conflict.

London buses played a vital role in supporting Britain and its allies with more than 1000 buses commandeered by the War Department for service on the front lines. Many of these were driven to France and Belgium, often by the same men who had driven them through London's streets.

It was the first use of motorised transport in a war and the converted 'battle buses' would travel at night, often in convoys of more than 70 vehicles, to transport troops to the front lines. They would take fresh troops out and return with the sick and wounded, or transport men leaving the trenches for rest periods. One entry in a driver's logbook states 'returned empty', a stark and chilling reminder of the many lives lost during the conflict.

ABOVE: The 'battle bus' is seen crossing Westminster Bridge. JOHN STILES

Chapter 18

It's a small world!

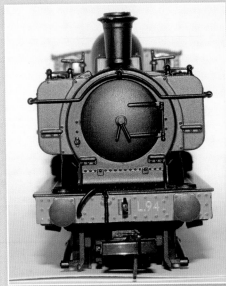

The Flour Mill's GWR prairie has, as we have seen, gone where no other member of the class has gone before, many times. In time for the Steam Back on the Met series of runs over London Underground's surface lines in spring 2013, as covered in Chapter 15, London Transport Museum brought out a model specially commissioned from Bachmann Europe, for sale at the event and its Covent Garden shop.

No. 5521 was by no means the first prairie tank to appear in OO scale, but it was certainly the first in London Transport maroon livery.

The model portrays No. 5521 as L150, but in the form in which it ran before the cab roof was lowered to fit in the tunnels.

The model is far above what you might imagine as a mere souvenir of Met 150. It has all the detailing you would expect from a major manufacturer, with the livery and lining superbly replicated.

The museum followed up the model of the red prairie by issuing another three special-edition OO gauge locomotives to mark the 150th anniversary of the Metropolitan Railway.

The pair of Class 20 Nos. 20189 and 20227, which were specially reliveried to take part in the abovementioned Steam Back on the Met series, were also commissioned from Bachmann. As with the GWR prairie, no examples ever became part of the LU fleet, and the models were very much a one-off for the Met 150 events.

No. 20227, which carried Railfreight red-stripe livery before the repaint, has a connection with the Underground. It had been frequently used for the delivery of brand new S-Stock trains from Derby to Neasden depot.

Although it did not appear in the 2013 or 2014 steam runs over the Underground, the museum also commissioned Bachmann to produce a model of GWR pannier No. 7752 in its latter-day and current London Transport livery as L94.

L94 hauled the final steam-hauled train on the Underground on June 6, 1971, and not only made the 10pm TV news, but also the front page of the Daily Telegraph.

Having been bitten by the OO modelling bug during Met 150, in September 2015 the museum issued another Bachmann model, a new Underground S-Stock set.

The motorised set, comprising four cars and including two driving cars, represent the units that made their debut on the Metropolitan Line in 2010 and show Aldgate as the destination.

*For details of prices and availability of these models, visit the Covent Garden museum's shop at www.ltmuseumshop.co.uk or telephone 020 7565 7295. ●

Chapter 19

Met 1 on tour

The star of Met 150 is also a roving ambassador for the company which began London Underground.

It is wrong to think of the Metropolitan Railway 150 celebrations as an exclusively London affair.

We have already seen how several heritage railways in England and Wales made significant contributions to the preparations for the ground-breaking event – the loan of the Beattie well tank for the test ruins, the restoration of Jubilee coach No. 353, Metropolitan Railway E class 0-4-4T running at 50mph.

When the deal to restore No.1, the centrepiece of the show, was agreed with Buckinghamshire Railway Centre, it was never the intention to use it purely for Met 150.

Under its 10-year loan, it would be made available for hire to other heritage lines, allowing the provinces to experience a little of the Metropolitan magic that had elevated the capital's tube system to the world stage.

After the phenomenally successful first public trips through the tunnels in January 2013, Met No. 1 returned to its home at the centre on February 17, 2013.

It was paired with Metropolitan Railway Dreadnought carriage No. 465 for a series of trips up and down one of the centre's two running lines.

Visitors who missed out on the draw to buy the Met 150 steam tickets at £150-180 per head in the January were able to ride behind

ABOVE: Met No. 1 in action at Quainton Road as seen from the southern footbridge. ROBIN JONES

No. 1 as many times as they liked during the day for a fraction of that amount.

Trevor England, chairman of the Vintage Carriages Trust based at Ingrow on the Keighley & Worth Valley Railway, formally handed the Dreadnought coach over to the Quainton Railway Society. In turn, he was presented with a painting of Met No. 1 hauling ▶ a teak train to cement a five-year loan deal for the recently revarnished coach.

BELOW: Met No. 1 returns to the centre's platform with the last train of the day on February 17, 2013. Metropolitan Railway Dreadnought coach No. 465 is coupled behind. ROBIN JONES

ABOVE: Trevor England, chairman of the Ingrow-based Vintage Carriages Trust, is presented with a painting of Metropolitan Railway No. 1 in service by Buckinghamshire Railway Centre trustees Andrew Bratton (left) and Tony Lyster. ROBIN JONES ABOVE RIGHT: Metropolitan Railway Dreadnought coach No. 465 back in London 'territory'. BIG AND LITTLE

ABOVE: The cloudless azure sky complements the striking maroon livery of Met No. 1 at Quainton Road. ROBIN JONES

ABOVE: A display of signs from E class No. 1's old Metropolitan Railway haunts inside the Buckinghamshire Railway Centre museum. ROBIN JONES

ABOVE: Not exactly Steam on the Met in 1995, but parallel running all the same: Met No. 1 heads a shuttle past the Vale Of Aylesbury Model Engineering Society's 7¼in gauge line at Quainton Road on February 17, 2013. ROBIN JONES

No. 465 is a nine-compartment third built in 1919, and is of a type that was in daily use through Quainton Road en route to Verney Junction. Special features on the Dreadnoughts are unusually wide footboards and curved tops to the doors to reduce the risk of damage if accidentally opened in tunnels. It is finished in London Transport's final 'dark brown' livery.

The carriage was retired from service in September 1961, when the tracks from Rickmansworth to Amersham were electrified, and in May 1963 the carriage was used in the Neasden cavalcade to celebrate the centenary of the Met.

The three Metropolitan Railway carriages owned by the Vintage Carriages Trust were initially purchased privately by David Kitton from London Transport for the then-proposed Westerham Valley Railway preservation project. When that scheme failed, and its volunteers migrated to the Kent & East Sussex Light Railway revival, the carriages were loaned to the Keighley & Worth Valley Railway in July 1965. Two of them formed part of the KWVR's reopening train in 1968. The VCT bought all three carriages from David in 1974.

February 17 was the first time one of the three surviving Dreadnought carriages had been seen in the London area since 1965.

BACK ON THE VALLEY – BUT AT 25MPH

The Severn Valley Railway's annual autumn steam gala is one of the big highlights of the enthusiast calendar, with crowds flocking to see, photograph and ride behind star guest locomotives.

In 2013, topping the bill at the September 20-22, 2013 event was Met No.1, partnered with Jubilee coach No. 353.

This visit was in part to thank the Severn Valley Railway for the use of its facilities for running in and the 50mph test run, as described in Chapter 12.

However, this time round, No. 1 had to keep to the permitted line speed of 25mph.

Met No. 1 had been earmarked to return to Quainton Road for a gala on October 6, but a change of plan saw it go straight to the Bodmin & Wenford Railway.

LEFT: Proudly carrying its Metropolitan Railway 150 badge on its chimney, Met No. 1 wowed the crowds at the Severn Valley Railway's 2013 autumn gala, along with Jubilee coach No. 353, behind which a pair of BR Mk.1 coaches are coupled. LEWIS MADDOX

BELOW: No. 1 crosses the Severn Valley Railway's Oldbury viaduct over Daniel's Mill with the 3.44pm Bridgnorth to Hampton Loade shuttle on September 21, 2013. EDWARD DYER

BODMIN BACK IN VICTORIAN TIMES

The first-ever visit of Metropolitan Railway E class 0-4-4T No. 1 to the Bodmin & Wenford Railway was one of the highlights of the Cornish line's October 12-13, 2013 Victorian gala – which saw three 19th-century locomotives in action.

The visit of No. 1 was a thank-you gesture for the loan in February the previous year of Bodmin-based LSWR Beattie well tank No. 30587 for, as outlined in Chapter 10, the series of trial overnight runs to see if it were feasible to run steam-hauled passenger trains through the modern Metropolitan Line tunnels.

The gala was preceded on October 11 by the launch into traffic of the magnificently restored and unique GWR First Class Family Saloon No. 248, which was built at Swindon in 1881.

Now owned by Bodmin & Wenford Railway Trust chairman, Alan Moore, it was previously used privately by Queen Victoria's son the Prince of Wales, the future Edward VII.

The coach, which was inspected by the young princes William and Harry when exhibited at Swindon in 1990, has been restored externally and internally by a team of craftsmen at Bodmin.

Two trains ran with the saloon, fitting in around the service trains. Firstly, Met No. 1 took it from Bodmin General to Bodmin Parkway and back, and the Beattie from Bodmin General to Boscarne and back.

Local TV and radio extensively covered the VIP launch on the day.

RIGHT: Victorian magnificence for the 21st century: GWR First Class Family Saloon No. 248 at Bodmin General. BRIAN ASTON

BELOW: Metropolitan Railway E class 0-4-4T No. 1 hauling the newly recommissioned GWR special saloon No. 248 at Charlie's Gate. BRIAN ASTON

During the gala, a vintage train comprising the special saloon and the line's GWR auto-coach ran an intensive service with the service train, featuring 11 departures from Bodmin General.

Motive power varied with combinations of Met No. 1 (built 1898), the well tank (1874), LSWR T9 4-4-0 No. 30120 (1898), and GWR 0-6-0 pannier No. 4612. What the four of them had in common was that they had all been restored to steam at Bill Parker's Flour Mill workshop at Bream.

A £3.50 premium was charged to ride in the special saloon, and on the Saturday it sold out.

The railways had actors dressed as various characters (Edward VII, Isambard Kingdom Brunel, Lillie Langtry) travelling on the trains, and the public were encouraged to dress in Victorian costume, and many of whom did.

SOUTHERN TOUR 2014

Met No. 1 visited the Mid Hants Railway in March 2014. It was run in on Thursday, March 6, before hauling public services during the ensuing three-day spring gala.

It headed a variety of services including a shuttle service using the line's Class 205 'Thumper' diesel electric multiple unit.

Met No. 1 then visited the Swindon and Cricklade Railway over the Easter weekend and for the line's April 26-27 steam gala.

Despite suffering a hot axlebox, it was repaired in time for the gala.

The locomotive next moved on loan to Didcot Railway Centre for the May Day Bank Holiday weekend.

Also in 2014, No. 1 visited the Barry Tourist Railway and ran there over the August Bank Holiday weekend.

RIGHT: Met No. 1 arrives at Ropley with the 2.40pm shuttle from Alresford on March 8, 2014, during the Mid Hants Railway's spring steam gala. HEC TATE*

ABOVE: No. 1 heads over the level crossing on the Didcot Railway Centre demonstration line. FRANK DUMBLETON

ABOVE: No. 1 runs round at Taw Valley Halt on the Swindon & Cricklade Railway on June 14, as it prepares to reattach to the stock for the run up to Hayes Knoll. HEC TATE*

RIGHT: Met No. 1 lines up alongside 1908-built GWR railmotor No. 98 at Didcot Railway Centre as its crew collects the token from Radstock North signalbox. Now unique, this railmotor is a link between the steam locomotive and the modern diesel multiple unit concepts and is therefore historically priceless. FRANK DUMBLETON

PURBECK GOES METROPOLITAN

The magic of the award-winning London underground steam trips extended to the Isle of Purbeck, when Metropolitan Railway E class 0-4-4T No. 1 became the star of the Swanage Railway's successful October 17-19, 2014 autumn steam gala.

No. 1 was joined by Severn Valley Railway-based WR pannier tank No. 1501, which was also making its first visit to the line for the gala.

More than 2000 people turned up to ride behind the pair and home-based Southern Railway U-class No. 31806 of 1928, GWR 0-6-2T No. 6695 and Bulleid Pacific No. 34070 *Manston*, operating to an intensive timetable including non-stop trains that didn't call at Herston and Harman's Cross.

Swanage Railway then general manager, Richard Jones, said: "Met No. 1 was the last steam locomotive built at the Neasden Works of the Metropolitan Railway, which was absorbed into London Transport during the 1930s. It's ironic that No. 1 has been turned on our turntable at Swanage as it was rescued from London Transport's Neasden depot.

BELOW: With the striking ruins of the Norman castle making for one of the most impressive backgrounds in the heritage sector, Met No. 1 departs from Corfe Castle en route to Swanage during the autumn 2014 gala. ANDREW PM WRIGHT

Chapter 20

Forever steam on the
Underground

A rural outpost of the London Underground, the Epping to Ongar extension of the Central line closed in 1994, recently it has been revived as the multiple award-winning Epping Ongar Railway.

The first scheme was proposed for a line to run from Stepney on the London & Blackwall Railway to Ongar in 1844, but it was not until 1858 that the Epping Railway came up with a successful route, running from Loughton to Ongar.

In 1862 the Epping Railway was absorbed into the Eastern Counties Railway and in the same year amalgamated with other companies to form the Great Eastern Railway.

The opening of the line, along with its stations at Chigwell Lane (now Debden), Theydon Bois, Epping, North Weald, Blake Hall and Ongar was celebrated at Ongar, where the first train was met by local dignitaries, a brass band and the Cadet Corps from Dr Clark's Grammar School, which fired a celebration volley as the first train arrived.

Goods traffic was very important. Ongar had one passenger platform, five sidings and a goods shed. The railway provided easy access to London's markets – very important for an agricultural local economy. Of particular importance was milk – between 1894 and 1899 milk traffic increased by 50% and from 1911 there was a dedicated milk train every weekday with a Saturday service was added in 1916. By 1918 some 5000 churns of milk (680,000 pints) of milk were being supplied to Stratford each week.

Following the end of the First World War, rail strikes, competition from road transport, the spread of refrigeration and a lack of investment in bulk handling facilities meant that the level of freight traffic diminished.

During the Thirties, two schemes were proposed to electrify the line. The first, in 1933, by the LNER did not go ahead because the company did not have the funds to implement it by itself. However, a New Works Programme proposed by the Government included plans to have the line to Ongar electrified by 1941. The Second World War saw the suspension of the programme but also a reduction in the services to Ongar, direct services to Liverpool Street reduced to operate at peak hours only, with a shuttle for off-peak services.

▶

BELOW: GWR 4-6-0 No. 4953 *Pitchford Hall* breaks the banner at North Weald to declare the 'new' Epping Ongar Railway open on May 24, 2012. ROBIN JONES

ABOVE: F6 tank engine No. 67218 waits to depart from Ongar, behind the long-demolished signalbox. EPPING ONGAR RAILWAY SOCIETY

ABOVE: Great Eastern Railway F5 2-4-2 tank No. 67202 at Epping shed in 1950, still providing sterling service in the early days of British Railways. EPPING ONGAR RAILWAY SOCIETY

After the end of the war, the Government prioritised infrastructure improvements and the Central Line extension reached Stratford on December 4, 1946 followed by Leytonstone on May 5, 1947. Steam trains shuttled between those stations and Ongar until December 14, 1947 when the steam/tube interchange moved to Woodford.

Following Nationalisation, the London Transport Executive inherited the former Central Railway assets, and from September 25, 1949, the branch passed into London Transport control.

Attempts were made during the Fifties to improve the steam service between Epping and Ongar. By September 1953, North Weald was the busiest station on the line on account of the staff and freight traffic going to and from the airfield. During the air shows there was a service every 15 minutes from Loughton.

ELECTRIFICATION AND RUNDOWN

Electrification of the line had been mooted in the New Works Programme and indeed in 1949 rails had been laid north of Epping. Despite space being set aside at Blake Hall for a substation, it was eventually decided to give the line 'light electrification' at a cost of £100,000. This provided for the traction power for the branch from Epping, which meant that the power available for tube trains was limited. At the same, Epping locomotive shed was closed, this now forming the extensive car park at that station.

In 1957, electric passenger trains were finally able to run to Ongar. A 20-minute passenger service was offered from Epping, although freight services continued to run with steam until 1962,

ABOVE: The final electric service on the line on September 30 1994, passes Blake Hall, the least patronised of all London Underground stations when it closed. EPPING ONGAR RAILWAY SOCIETY

before being taken over by diesels, typically coming down the branch by night after passenger services had finished.

As passenger numbers fell, from October 17, 1966 Blake Hall station was closed on Sundays and a reduced weekday timetable implemented. In 1970 the Epping to Ongar section of the Central Line was operating at a loss of £100,000 per year and London Transport started formal closure proceedings. The Secretary of State refused the closure order in 1972 but did not provide any grant to make up the shortfall. In 1976 staffing was reduced on the line, which led to a further noticeable drop in passenger numbers.

London Transport tried to get a further closure order from the Secretary of State in May 1980 – but this move sparked the creation of the Epping and Ongar Railway Society and Epping Forest Railway Ltd – both aimed at saving the line in order to operate it as a heritage railway.

With just six passengers a day, Blake Hall station was the least used on the entire Underground network and was closed on October 31, 1981.

An all-day service ran from October 30, 1989 and Ongar gained a large illuminated roundel – both aimed to attract passengers. The increase in service, however, failed to attract sufficient custom and by April 1991 the branch line was back to peak hours only.

In the early 1990s, with the threat of closure looming once more, the Ongar Railway Preservation Society was formed to acquire and operate the line using preserved 1960 and 1962 tube stock as well as preserved steam and diesel locomotives.

With passenger numbers having fallen to around 100 a day, London Transport again applied to the Secretary of State, this time suggesting the sale of the branch as an operational railway, to a third party. After September 30, 1994, passenger services over the 6½ miles between Epping and Ongar were withdrawn. With the sale later approved by Labour's transport minister, Glenda Jackson.

UNDERGROUND RECLAIMS 'LOST' ONGAR BRANCH

London Transport 'took over' its former Epping to Ongar branch for eight days as part of the celebrations to mark the 150th anniversary of the Underground.

The heritage line held its first steam gala on June 21-24 and June 28-July 1, 2013.

Topping the guest list were Met No. 1, GWR small prairie L150 and GNR N2 0-6-2T No. 1744, the latter running on former LNER metals and carrying a special headboard marking the Golden Jubilee of its owner the Gresley Society.

GWR prairie No. 4141, a former Old Oak Common engine that worked at Paddington, was renumbered to 6141. A heritage set of coaches was formed, comprising the restored Metropolitan Railway carriage No. 353 and two Metropolitan Railway

RIGHT: Met No. 1 in action on July 30, 2013, during the Met 150 celebrations on the 'lost' part of the Underground. BRIAN SHARPE

SAVED TWICE

The Ongar Railway Preservation Society's bid to take over the line was rejected by the Government in favour of one from property developer Pilot Developments, which had promised to restart commuter services using a preserved diesel multiple unit in the first instance, but failed to deliver, one reason given being the lack of access to Epping's Central Line station. Pilot removed the electric rails, saying at the time they had been undermined by burrowing rabbits. Earlier, a Pilot spokesman infamously said that the railway could host visits by steam locomotives, with A3 Pacific No. 4472 Flying Scotsman having its chimney hinged so it could pass beneath the M11, which had clearance for only the much lower tube stock. Needless to say, Pilot Developments quickly lost credibility among the enthusiast fraternity.

However, Pilot director Roger Wright, who had the smallest stake in the company, and had ridden on the line on the last day of services in 1994, became the hero of the day. Firstly he vetoed a plan to regauge the line to 5ft so it could use imported Finnish steam locomotives, and then he bought the freehold.

The former Essex bus magnate then bought two Great Western locomotives – 4-6-0 No. 4953 Pitchford Hall and large prairie No. 4141 – and embarked on a major process of renovation of Ongar and North Weald stations, extending the platforms from four- to six-coach capability turning the clock back to the steam era.

Roger's much-welcomed investment and enthusiasm bore fruit on May 24, 2012, when A VIP opening day was held at North Weald in advance of the resumption of public services at a gala the following weekend.

At 2.45pm, Pitchford Hall broke a banner across the track to declare the railway open for business again. Also in steam was GWR pannier No. 6430, on loan from the Llangollen Railway, which was overhauling No. 4141 in readiness for its Ongar debut.

The line was still unable to share the station at Epping, but trains ran to a point at Coopersale, in the middle of an outlier

ABOVE: Yet another type of GWR pannier makes its debut on the Underground in the heritage era: Hugh Shipton's auto-fitted 64XX, a variant of the 57XX but with the ability to haul autotrains in push-pull mode, at North Weald station on loan from the Llangollen Railway on May 24, 2012. ROBIN JONES

ABOVE: Epping Ongar Railway proprietor Roger Wright interviewed for TV at the VIP launch of the 'reborn' line on May 24, 2012. ROBIN JONES

of Epping Forest, pending the building of a dedicated western terminus station for heritage trains.

Such were the sweeping changes that had been enacted under Roger's brief ownership that the railway scooped three major honours, the Ian Allan Publishing Heritage Railway of the Year Award in the 2012 National Railway Heritage Awards, the Volunteers Award for the work undertaken at its 1865 Grade II listed Ongar terminus including the restoration of the footwarmer hut, porters' room and the signalbox structure, as well as the Heritage Railway Association's 2012 Railway of the Year award.

ABOVE: The fabric of the original stations on the line, all of which survive, including the Ongar terminus seen here, have been painstakingly restored under Roger Wright's ownership. ROBIN JONES

'Dreadnought' coaches from the Twenties, first-class carriage No. 509 and brake No. 427, loaned from Vintage Carriages Trust at Ingrow. A Fifties British Railways' maroon suburban coach on loan from the North

Norfolk Railway completed the set.

Also in steam was GWR 4-6-0 No. 4953 Pitchford Hall, and passengers were able to connect to the Central Line at Epping via railway owner Roger Wright's beautifully

restored fleet of original London Transport buses operating shuttles from North Weald.

The two-weekend gala, the biggest event in the heritage line's history, was hailed as a major success as we closed for press.

ABOVE: The Flour Mill's maroon-liveried prairie tank L150 (5521) joined the gala action, and is seen on June 21, 2013 about to depart North Weald for Ongar. CLIFF THOMAS

ABOVE: Met No. 1 in gala action with the Epping Ongar railway's Mk.2 coaching set. MARTIN PEARSON

A TUBE TRAIN RUNS AGAIN TO ONGAR!

ABOVE: On September 26, 2014, EOR supremo Roger Wright presents LU managing director Mike Brown with a replica 0.0km posy sign, from which the distance of every piece of London Underground track is still measured, even though the Ongar branch is now privately owned. ANDY BARR **ABOVE RIGHT:** Point of origin: the 0.0km zero point at the Ongar bufferstop, from which London Underground distances are calculated. ROBIN JONES

ABOVE: The Flour Mill's maroon-liveried prairie tank L150 (5521) joined the gala action, and is seen on June 21, 2013 about to depart North Weald for Ongar. CLIFF THOMAS

LEFT: Met No. 1 heads a freight working through Coopersale's leafy glades, not exactly the stereotypical image of London Underground. EOR

ABOVE: Look no pickup rails! The preserved Cravens' set is propelled through the woods near Coopersale, a journey it made several times a day under its own power until the line closed in 1994. EOR **ABOVE RIGHT:** Two Schomas bring the 1960 Craven set into North Weald while Met No. 1 waits for the next northbound departure. The person on the bufferbeam of the diesel is exchanging the single line staff to allow the train to proceed from North Weald to the EOR's current terminal point at Coopersale. ANDY BARR

In the autumn of 2014, 20 years after a 1960 London Underground tube train ran to the system's north-eastern extremity of Ongar, it made the journey again. Only this time round, there were no electric rails!

Following closure of the branch in 1994, a group of Ongar Railway Preservation Society members bought 1960 stock tube cars Nos. 3906, 4927 and 3907 and formed a company, Cravens Heritage Trains Limited to restore them. The set has been used for tours on the Underground since 1995.

The set was moved from Ruislip depot and taken to the heritage line via the Underground for a special End of Tube gala on the Epping Ongar railway on September 26-28. It arrived at Epping on the Central Line under its own power – but to cross the link on to the Epping Ongar Railway, and operate services between North Weald and Ongar, it had to be top-and tailed by four London Underground Schoma diesels, part of the system's engineering fleet.

It was one of the first, and last, times that these locomotives would haul passengers as they were be progressively converted to 'battery locomotive' configuration for continuing use by the Underground engineering team.

The stop blocks between the end of LU metals and the EOR were removed on the evening of September 25 to allow the unit in.

Representing the steam era during the gala was Met No. 1. During the weekend it ran both passenger workings and a short goods set made up of a Rectank, a London Transport ballast wagon and half brake van No. 578, the latter two being brought in from their Buckinghamshire Railway Centre home.

At Ongar on September 26, Underground managing director, Mike Brown, unveiled a 'zero post' 0.0km plate that had traditionally occupied a site by the bufferstops at the station and from which point, track measurement across the London Underground network traditionally took place – and still does to this day, despite the closure and sell-off.

On the Saturday of the event, special runs of the Cravens took passengers right up the boundary with the Underground, the closest that passengers from Ongar have been to Epping in two decades.

Demands for tickets was so great over the three days that passengers could be seen inside the three cars 'strap-hanging' in traditional commuter style!

EPPING ONGAR RAILWAY REACHES EPPING... ALMOST

On April 18, 2015, the heritage line extend its running line by 900 yards from its Coopersale Common western stopping point to its current stop board at Stonards Hill, in time for both that year's April 18-19 spring diesel gala and the line's own 150th anniversary celebrations on April 24-26. The westernmost point for passenger services was renamed Epping Forest in the 2015 timetable.

This 'new' passenger-carrying section of the line was the subject of a substantial amount of engineering work last year in preparation for the 2014 End of Tube event and saw extensive sleeper renewal, the cutting back of vegetation and dropping of ballast.

On April 24, 150 years to the day of the opening of the branch, it welcomed guests from the Epping Ongar Railway Volunteer Society; children from the Chipping Ongar Primary School; local MP Eric Pickles, Secretary of State for communities and local government in the coalition government, and Tony Boyce chairman of Epping Forest District Council among others.

At 10.40am a packed train arrived at Ongar from North Weald to be greeted by flag-waving children and cheers from the crowd to the accompaniment of a brass band.

After speeches were made, a commemorative plaque was unveiled at Ongar station.

The official ceremony was followed by a three-day Eastern-themed steam gala celebrating steam locomotives that would have run over lines operated by the GER and its successors the LNER and BR.

The event featured guests J72 No. 69023 Joem, Y7 0-4-0T No. 785 and N2 0-6-2T No. 1774.

Roger Wright said: "When I see the tremendous support there is for the railway, especially after we have nudged that much closer to Epping station, I look forward to the next 150 years with pride and to the day when we have a connection with the Underground at Epping."

Although it was never part of Metro-land, the Epping to Ongar branch is an archetypal example of one of those outposts of the Underground that ventured into the rural shires surrounding the capital. As such, it could not be made to pay, and became a very rare example of an Underground line to be closed.

Now it is making a major contribution to London's transport heritage, being the only standard gauge steam line directly on the doorstep of the capital. Thanks to Roger Wright, it has so much going for it, and we look forward to the day when it connects with Central Line services at Epping, in some shape or form.

Imagine being able to use your Oyster card to hop off the Tube anywhere in London, and be able to change on to a steam train within an hour. The potential for tourism is enormous. ●

ABOVE: Visitors J52 No. 69053 and N2 No. 1774 face each other at Ongar during the 150th anniversary celebrations in April 2015. tNEVILLE WELLINGS

Chapter 21

Watford Metropolitan
steam twilight

The 90th anniversary celebrations of Watford's Metropolitan Line may have been the last visit of a steam train to the town's Underground station as the new Croxley Link will reroute services.

ABOVE: One of the iconic scenes from the first Steam on the Met series between 1999-2000 was the sight of steam locomotives crossing the bridge over the Grand Union Canal while running out of Watford Metropolitan Line station. On Sunday, February 13, Metropolitan Railway E class 0-4-4T No. 1 raised a head of steam as it headed its train towards Croxley. This view will be lost when the Croxley Link reroutes the line into Watford High Street. JOHN TITLOW

The Underground steam programme in 2015 comprised a weekend of runs between Harrow-on-the-Hill, Watford and Chesham. The weekend celebrated the 90th anniversary of Watford's Metropolitan Line station in Cassiobury Park Avenue. However, the hugely successful event may well have seen the final steam trains to run into Watford's tube station, as it is soon to be rendered redundant by the opening of the new Coxley Link.

The professionalism and expertise of the Flour Mill workshop was again praised after steam returned to London Underground metals in magnificent style.

With only days of the eagerly awaited Watford 90 series of trips from Harrow-on-the-Hill and Watford to Chesham on September 12-13 to go, Flour Mill staff worked round the clock to rectify an historic fault with the regulation of Metropolitan Railway E class 0-4-4T No. 1.

The regulator was taken apart five times in the 10 days before the weekend specials and, after each time it was reassembled, the 1898-built locomotive was steam tested again. The final time, it passed with flying colours.

Following on from the stupendous success of the award-winning Met 150 celebrations,

running steam trains on the Underground between timetabled daily electric services has become somewhat of an annual feature, and a very popular one too.

However, it very nearly did not happen in 2015. As the preserved Cravens tube stock unit was making its way back over the Central Line from the Epping Ongar Railway's End of Tube gala in September 2014, a shoebeam fractured and part of it fell on to the track.

Placing safety first, London Underground immediately banned the movement of all heritage stock over its system until an enquiry into the incident was held. As a result plans to ▶

ABOVE: In a delightful scene that could have come straight out of a Metroland guide of the Thirties, the driver of GWR 2-6-2T L150 (5521) waves back at two young fans on the platform of Chorleywood station on September 13. JOHN TITLOW

ABOVE: Met No. 1 stands at Watford waiting to depart with the 3.10pm to Chesham on September 12. ROBIN JONES

ABOVE: Met No. 1 approaches Rickmansworth with the 3.10pm from Watford on September 13. JOHN TITLOW

ABOVE: The special vintage pop-up team room at Watford station. ROBIN JONES

run steam in the summer of 2015 through the tunnels between Ealing Broadway and High Street Kensington were postponed.

However, once the recommendations from that enquiry had been implemented, Watford 90 was allowed to go ahead.

BELOW: Prairie L150 passes Rickmansworth with the 4pm from Chesham on September 13. JOHN TITLOW

Just as with the Met 150 specials, the train included the Bluebell Railway's Chesham set, Jubilee coach No. 353, milk van No 3, and No. 12 Sarah Siddons, which was tucked in behind No. 1 on the outward journeys.

Providing traction in top-and-tail mode for the return trips was GWR prairie L150 (5521).

The weekend marked the 90th anniversary of the opening of Watford's Metropolitan Line station on November 4, 1925, with Met electric rather than steam services to Baker Street – and the first locomotive to haul a passenger train into it was Sarah Siddons.

For the first few months, the LNER ran steam services from Watford Metropolitan to Marylebone. However, patronage proved

ABOVE: Met No. 1 approaches Chorleywood with the 3.10pm from Watford on September 12. JOHN TITLOW

disappointing because the station lies a mile from Watford town centre.

STEAM TAKES OVER THE BRANCH!

For the September 12-13, 2015 series, between 11am until 4.30pm, normal passenger services between Chalfont & Latimer and from Chesham were suspended. Timetabled trains to and from Chesham were instead diverted to Amersham, from where a replacement bus service was in operation to Chesham.

The first train of each day ran from Harrow at 11.01am to Chesham and back to Watford, arriving at 12.30pm. The next service was a Watford-Chesham round trip, leaving at 1.10pm and returning at 2.30pm. The third service ran from Watford at 3.10pm and returned from Chesham to Harrow, arriving at 4.41pm.

A novel idea for the weekend, and a first for the Underground steam series, was a vintage pop-up tea room on the platform at Watford station.

Organiser London Transport Museum teamed up with Tea Darling, a firm that arranges quirky and tailor-made vintage tea parties, to create an 'instant' tea room, where, for a special supplement, steam train passengers were able to sip tea brewed in beautiful teapots on the platform and enjoy Victoria sponge cake served on ornate crockery.

A gramophone played while the kettle boiled to recreate the Metroland atmosphere of a bygone era of suburban London.

RIGHT: The empty coaching stock movement into Harrow-on-the-Hill on the morning of September 13. JOHN TITLOW

Andy Barr, head of heritage operations at the Covent Garden museum, said that the weekend had been "absolutely superb".

He praised the work done by Geoff Phelps, backed up by Dennis Howells, owner of 94XX No. 9466, in ensuring that No. 1 was ready to steam, after their 11th-hour work to solve the regulator problem. "Without the work they did, Met No. 1 would not have run," he said. "The locomotives performed absolutely magnificently."

As it was, No. 1 turned in a brilliant performance, belying its vintage. It easily hauled the consist up the 1-in-66 gradients from Chalfont & Latimer and Chesham and the 1-in-105 between Rickmansworth and Chalfont.

Despite having *Sarah Siddons* coupled immediately behind, traction from the electric locomotive was not needed on most of the trips, the exception being when No. 1 had to slow down for a quarter of a mile at two points to minimise a fire risk. An emergency team had been placed on standby in case of any problems and quickly dealt with two very minor incidents.

ABOVE: GWR prairie L150 departs from Chesham with a flourish at the head of the 4pm to Harrow-on-the-Hill on September 12. ROBIN JONES

Andy said that the 12-mile 40-minutes-each-way route presented the steam drivers with several challenges, not least of all the 10mph restriction on entering the Chesham terminus. Despite climbing the gradient into the town, the locomotive had to reduce speed, without coming to a stop.

THE CROXLEY LINK

However, the Watford 90 trips may have been the last steam specials into Watford ▶

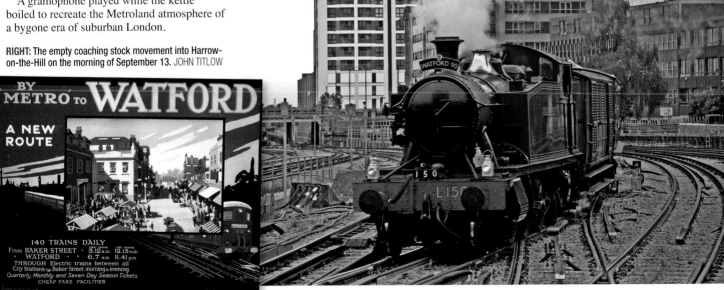

ABOVE: The 2pm from Chesham runs through Rickmansworth on September 13. JOHN TITLOW

Underground station, although at the time of writing, Andy Barr said that the organiser may seek to run one last trip there.

In 1994, the old ambition to extend the Metropolitan Line into Watford town centre was revived by London Regional Transport with proposals to run the line to Watford Junction.

Now the station is set to be bypassed by the Croxley Rail Link, which involves connecting the Metropolitan Line to the disused Watford & Rickmansworth

Railway line and reinstating the 1¼-mile Croxley Green branch to Watford High Street.

That line, opened in 1912, was closed by British Rail in 1996 because of low passenger numbers.

On July 24, 2013 the Secretary of State for transport issued a Transport and Works Order granting the necessary planning permissions, access rights and land transfers for the link, which will see Watford Met station closed to passengers.

The new arrangement will see the lines under Network Rail control, but with London Underground running the electric services over them.

However, the line into Watford's tube station is likely to remain operational as a siding. ●

ABOVE: With the current isolated from adjacent power supplies, the group of volunteers and drivers who made Watford 90 possible stand in Ruislip Depot at the end of the weekend's successful trips. ANDY BARR

ABOVE: Headed by Met No. 1, the special is seen after passing through Chalfont & Latimer on September 12. JOHN TITLOW

ABOVE: Met No. 1 heads the 3.10pm from Watford over the last few hundred yards into Chesham on September 12. ROBIN JONES RIGHT: GWR prairie L150, a sub class by virtue of its cut-down cab, on shed at Ruislip depot. ANDY BARR